IT'S **YOUR** BUSINESS

IT'S *YOUR* BUSINESS

183 ESSENTIAL TIPS THAT WILL TRANSFORM YOUR SMALL BUSINESS

JJ RAMBERG

With Lisa Everson & Frank Silverstein

BUSINESS PLUS

NEW YORK   BOSTON

Business Plus
Hachette Book Group
237 Park Avenue
New York, NY 10017

www.HachetteBookGroup.com

Printed in the United States of America

RRD-C

First Edition: October 2012
10 9 8 7 6 5 4 3 2 1

Business Plus is an imprint of Grand Central Publishing.
The Business Plus name and logo are trademarks of Hachette Book Group, Inc.

The Hachette Speakers Bureau provides a wide range of authors for speaking events. To find out more, go to www.hachettespeakersbureau.com or call (866) 376-6591.

The publisher is not responsible for websites (or their content) that are not owned by the publisher.

Library of Congress Cataloging-in-Publication Data
Ramberg, J. J. (Jennifer J.)
    It's your business : 183 essential tips that will transform your small business / by JJ Ramberg ; with Lisa Everson and Frank Silverstein. — 1st ed.
        p. cm.
    Includes index.
    ISBN 978-1-4555-0900-3 (trade pbk.)
    1. Small business—Management.   2. New business enterprises—Management.
I. Everson, Lisa.   II. Silverstein, Frank, 1956–   III. Title.
    HD62.7.R35 2012
    658.02'2—dc23
                                                                    2012008281

For Scott Leon

CONTENTS

INTRODUCTION   ix

CHAPTER ONE—Finding Your Funding   1
Attracting investors, getting loans,
and tapping other sources of capital

CHAPTER TWO—Getting It Off the Ground   19
Launching a new company, product, or service

CHAPTER THREE—Being the Leader   42
Understanding your business and yourself

CHAPTER FOUR—Creating Your Team   72
Hiring, firing, evaluating, and other HR issues

CHAPTER FIVE—Managing People   95
How to get the best from your employees

CHAPTER SIX—Closing the Sale   116
Selling your goods or services

CHAPTER SEVEN—Cultivating Customers   146
Getting and keeping your customers

CHAPTER EIGHT—Getting Your Message Out There   188
Marketing your company and courting
the press

CHAPTER NINE—Building Relationships   215
   Networking and communication

CHAPTER TEN—Controlling Costs   235
   How to keep expenses in check

CHAPTER ELEVEN—Running the Office   249
   Keeping things running smoothly

ABOUT THE AUTHORS   269

ACKNOWLEDGMENTS   273

CONTRIBUTOR INDEX   277

COMPANY INDEX   281

INTRODUCTION

My name is JJ Ramberg, and I am an entrepreneur. I was born into a family of entrepreneurs. I'm married to an entrepreneur. I host a national television show about entrepreneurs for an audience of entrepreneurs. And, when I'm not doing that, I help run my own business, which I co-founded with my brother, Ken Ramberg, called GoodSearch.com. Many of my closest friends are entrepreneurs. And my guess is if you just picked up this book, you've got a good streak of entrepreneurship running through your veins too.

This book is a collection of some of the smartest, most practical, and easy-to-understand business advice out there. It's straightforward information that you don't need a business school degree to understand, and you don't need to be a *Fortune* 500 company to use. And believe me, thanks to these past six years of hosting *Your Business* on MSNBC, I've heard it all and seen it all—in action. This stuff works. Period. It's worked for the people who figured it out and, in many cases, it's worked for me at my own company. While some of it is just plain common sense, much of it is highly original and extremely clever.

Since I started hosting MSNBC's *Your Business* in 2006, my colleagues and I have interviewed thousands of entrepreneurs to find out what they've learned about running their own companies. And honestly, no two individuals are alike. I've spoken with many different kinds of business owners, from sole proprietors working out of their own basements to people who pay the salaries of hundreds of employees working in large industrial facilities. I've met people funded by venture capitalists risking millions, angel investors risking hundreds of thousands, and plenty more who have funded their own ventures with nothing more than their life savings or a second mortgage on their home. And when you look at the industries they represent, they are all over the map. A random sample might include a dry cleaner in Pittsburgh, a tech start-up in Seattle, a restaurant in Manhattan, a real estate firm in Phoenix, a headhunter in New Orleans, a hot-air balloon operator in Napa, a dogsled-ride company in Aspen, a bank in Boston, a wedding planner in Chicago… the list is very, very long. But the common denominator is that each of these small business owners has had to confront and solve many different kinds of problems in all areas of business in order to survive and grow.

No matter where we are or what business we are in, I have found that there is one true quality that all of us entrepreneurs share—*we are a very determined bunch!* Even in the heart of the 2008 recession, I met people who simply did not have the words "I give up" in their vocabulary. We are people who, when you tell us "No!" we think "No for now." Tell us "Impossible!" and what we hear is "Impossible for now." We are go-getters who make things happen for ourselves, for our employees, and for our communities.

We are a very practical group and we generally don't settle. We are always on the lookout for the fastest, simplest, least wasteful, and most efficient way to get the best results for the least effort, money, and resources. We also don't spend a lot of time regretting our mistakes. In fact, many of our best ideas have come to us as lessons learned from huge mistakes.

And those ideas, those tips, those hard-earned insights are what we've collected and organized into this book.

As both a reporter/writer of this book and a self-employed entrepreneur, I've found myself in the position of receiving and then using much of the advice collected here. Receiving it—as a journalist with a national audience of small business owners—and then using it in the day-to-day operation of my own business, GoodSearch. I cannot tell you how often I've come away from one of my interviews with scribbles on the side of my notebook, reminding me to try out what that person is doing when I get back home to GoodSearch. These scribbles run the gamut from how to change someone's no into a yes (see Tips #101 and #102) to how to stand (literally—where exactly to put my feet!) when I'm giving a presentation (see Tip #40).

This book is basically a detailed look into these scribbles. It's filled with all of those tricks of the trade that people who are in the trenches every day—people who are doing the things all small business owners do, such as hiring people, developing pricing schedules, and negotiating deals—have created to help them with these tasks. Many are things that we're not doing because we just didn't think of them before. Many are things we know we should be doing but haven't had the time to figure out how. We'll tell you how.

I've learned a great deal from the advice we've collected. For example, in Tip #115, Josh Brookhart of TZG Partners provides insight on getting your customers to give you feedback on a product launch. As you'll see, I fortuitously spoke to Josh a week before a new GoodSearch launch and it totally changed the way we handled the introduction with our users. Other times I didn't get the advice before doing something, but immediately changed my practices once I heard it. For example,

Katherine Corp's Tip #109 has completely informed the way I talk to customers and potential partners.

This book is written with two of the producers of *Your Business*—Lisa Everson and Frank Silverstein. You can imagine, with thousands of interviews under our belt, we had an enormous pool of tips and advice to choose from. But we were picky in deciding which ones to include. Every single tip in this book is practical, actionable, easy to implement, and will help your business succeed. You can read one and make the change in your business that very day! We ran each tip by our informal focus group of small business owners to make sure their reaction was, "Wow, that's so smart, I have to start doing that in my company." Or, "Wow, I can't believe I'm not doing that already!"

Keep in mind, this not a comprehensive how-to-start-and-grow-your-business kind of book. If you're looking for that, there are plenty of books out there that fill that need. We clearly do not cover every single thing you need to know to run a business, and we didn't try.

What we did set out to do is put together a collection of "aha" moments—those magical discoveries in your business where you think, "Oh, that's a much better way to do it!" Most of these tips are not big-picture—they're very focused and very actionable. And, they're all easy to digest and quick to read.

Using myself as the prime example, most entrepreneurs do not have the luxury of time. My co-authors are always making fun of me, saying that I'm usually in such a hurry that when I call them, I simply say, "Hi, it's J," instead of "JJ," saving exactly one second. To that end, we decided not to spend ten pages on a piece of advice when we could get the point across in one paragraph.

You don't need to read this book in the order it was

written—and as a matter of fact, you probably shouldn't. Poke around. Flip open to a page and see what you find. Or, if you're focusing on an area of your business right now, head over to that section. If you have a meeting with your sales team coming up, go straight to chapter 6 on "Closing the Sale"; if you're wondering about your management style, go to chapter 3, "Being the Leader." Or, if you're just starting your company, you may want to begin with chapter 2 and read on to see how others are getting things right.

I started my company, GoodSearch.com, in 2005. It was a typical start-up, founded out of my one-bedroom apartment in New York City. GoodSearch is a socially responsible company that empowers people to turn their everyday actions into ways to do good. Each time someone searches the Internet, shops online, or dines out, a donation is made to their favorite charity or school. More than 15 million people have used GoodSearch, and we've raised around $10 million for good causes. Together with my brother and co-founder, Ken, I've dealt with all of the issues we touch on in this book. I've had to contemplate what kind of funding to get, how to fire someone, how to find office space, and how to get potential partners who had never heard of us to take a meeting. After five years of running the company ourselves, we hired Scott Garell, the former president of Ask.com, to be our CEO, at which time we dealt with issues of how to grow at the right speed. You'll hear a lot about my experiences as an entrepreneur in the following pages. Throughout our research and writing, I have used many, many of the tips in my own business. I'm quite sure you will do the same!

JJ Ramberg

A NOTE ON QR CODES

You'll notice throughout the book that we've added QR codes to some of the tips. Grab your phone and if you don't have a QR code reader, get one from the iTunes App Store or Android Market. We like Paperlinks, Scan, and RedLaser. Once you scan one of the codes with the reader, you'll be taken to a web page.

We have amassed six years' worth of videos from *Your Business*, and this gives us a way to share the best of them with you. Some of these codes will take you to segments going into more detail about the tip you're reading. Others will take you to a segment we filmed on the featured small business owner or expert that focuses on another piece of advice we learned from them.

We're thrilled that technology has allowed us to truly marry the show and this book. We hope you enjoy the segments!

Scan to see a video

IT'S **YOUR** BUSINESS

CHAPTER ONE

FINDING YOUR FUNDING

Attracting investors, getting loans, and tapping other sources of capital

TIP #1	Four must-haves for your elevator pitch	2
TIP #2	Do's and don'ts of meeting an investor	4
TIP #3	Sell your company—not the product—to investors	5
TIP #4	Don't choose investors based on valuation alone	6
TIP #5	Don't set a valuation during your friends-and-family round of funding	7
TIP #6	Borrow through peer-to-peer lending	9
TIP #7	Barter, don't buy	11
TIP #8	Ask your suppliers for funds	12
TIP #9	Ask your customers for payment up front	13
TIP #10	Have a bank loan application strategy	15
TIP #11	Find a market for the stuff you're throwing out	16
TIP #12	Be ready with a photo pitch on your phone	17

TIP #1
Four must-haves for your elevator pitch

On *Your Business*, nearly every week we have a segment called "The Elevator Pitch." Some are highly polished and some are quite raw. So we asked Brian Halligan to give us some advice on how to make sure your pitch is a home run.

As a venture capitalist, Brian has listened to many elevator pitches. As an entrepreneur and the founder of HubSpot in Boston, pitching for money is second nature. The most successful pitches, he says, include what he calls PATS:

> P—Show your **Passion** for your idea—don't hide it.
> A—**Ask** for a number—be specific: how much you want and how you will use it.
> T—Show **Traction**—website visitors increasing, early orders, press coverage, etc.
> S—Make **Sense**—rehearse it in front of the mirror and communicate your message clearly.

As small business owners, we often get so excited about our idea that we talk too long or give too much detail in an elevator pitch. So here is a simple worksheet for you to fill out:

> **Explanation:** One line saying what your company does: _____
> **Traction:** What statistics can you show to illustrate the upward success of your idea: _____
> **Size:** How big can your company become: _____
> **Ask:** What are you asking for: _____

Now take all of that information and put it into a paragraph and present it to someone who knows nothing about your business. Ask them if they now understand what you do, how successful you've been, and your potential for growth. Once you've got that down, stand in front of a mirror and practice, practice, practice so that you can deliver this pitch with passion and clarity. Remember, with a busy person, you've often only got one shot to impress them!

Added tip: David S. Rose, chairman of New York Angels, says you never know how much time someone is going to give you. So have an elevator pitch ready for every scenario: twenty seconds, one minute, five minutes, twenty minutes, and one hour.

TIP #2
Do's and don'ts of meeting an investor

Don't waste a good introduction with a poor follow-up. Too many people squander the opportunity to follow up with a potential investor once they've been introduced in a casual setting.

Mark Suster, a partner at GRP Partners, the largest venture-capital firm in Southern California, gave us this list of what to say and what *not* to say:

What NOT to say:

- "Can you please check out my website and let me know your thoughts?"
- "Here is my phone number, call me when you have time to talk."

Investors are busy and are inundated with requests from people to "check out their company." If you put the ball in their court, you'll likely never hear from them.

What TO say:

- "Would you mind if the next time I'm in town I e-mailed you to see if you had thirty minutes for a coffee?"
- "I know that you're very busy—would you mind if I asked for an intro to a junior member of your team to start a dialogue?"
- "I know my company may not be in the industry you focus on—do you know any angels who might be interested in our space?"

Take things into your own hands. This way you control the next step and can ensure that it happens.

TIP #3
Sell your company—not the product—to investors

Customers and investors have very different interests in your business. People often come on "The Elevator Pitch" segment of *Your Business* and spend the entire time talking about how great their product is. While that might get them a new customer, it does not necessarily get them a new investor.

Howard Morgan, managing partner at First Round Capital in New York, says that this is a common mistake and easily fixed. He says that entrepreneurs need to remember that when they are pitching investors, they're not pitching the *product* (as they would to a potential client or customer), they are pitching *shares* of the company. For example, when the company Public-Stuff (which provides outsourced 311 services to local governments) pitched their idea to Howard, the founders showed their product and it was, no doubt, intriguing. But Howard was more interested in learning how they would monetize the product and get the buy-in of their heavily politicized target customers.

Bottom line: It's important to talk about what drives the share value. This of course includes the product benefits, but also other things, such as your team, the marketplace, and your marketing plan. You need to be focused not on why the *product* is so great but on why your *company* is so great.

TIP #4
Don't choose investors based on valuation alone

It's not just the amount of money you get but whom you get it from that makes the biggest difference. When you're looking for funding, while it may be tempting to go with the investor who will give you the most money or the best deal in terms of valuation, New York–based Jason Goldberg, who has founded four tech companies including Fab.com (and sold two), says you shouldn't give in to that temptation. He says, when you are deciding whom to take money from, you should, in addition to the valuation, consider the following:

1. Are your business goals truly aligned? Here are the questions to ask yourself and your investors to see if you are on the same page:

- Do you want to grow quickly or build at a slow and steady pace?
- Do you want to sell the company soon or build a large business with hundreds of employees?
- Are you the person to run the company or should you bring in a CEO once you reach a certain scale?

2. Do you like working together and do you feel comfortable sharing your issues and getting advice from these people?

According to Jason, in the long run you'll be much happier basing your decision on the answers to those questions than the valuation question. Remember, once you take money from someone, you're in it with them for the long haul!

TIP #5
Don't set a valuation during your friends-and-family round of funding

Problem: You're raising a round of money from friends and family to get your company off the ground, but you don't know how much of the company you should give away to them.

Solution: Don't make that decision right now! David S. Rose, chairman of New York Angels and a serial entrepreneur, says that you can figure that out later. How? Give your friends and family convertible notes with a 20 percent discount on the next round. OK, OK…I realize that likely sounded completely confusing, so let me explain.

When your best friend gives you $5,000, don't give her a percentage of the company. Instead, make it a loan that will be converted to equity if and when you raise your next round of funding. Then, when you raise the next round (presumably from more sophisticated investors), the company's value will be set during the negotiation between you and this second round of investors. At that point, your best friend's loan will turn into equity. But since she took the risk of betting on you from the start, she'll get 20 percent more for her $5,000 than someone who put in $5,000 in this round.

Still confusing? Here's a simplified worksheet to clarify things.

Round #1:
Mom: $10,000 convertible note
Brother: $5,000 convertible note
Best friend: $5,000 convertible note

Round #2: Company is worth $500,000 after the investment

New investor: $100,000—now owns 20 percent of equity

Mom: now owns 2.4 percent of company ($10,000 converted into equity plus 20 percent more)

Brother: now owns 1.2 percent of company ($5,000 converted into equity plus 20 percent more)

Best friend: now owns 1.2 percent of company ($5,000 converted into equity plus 20 percent more)

TIP #6
Borrow through peer-to-peer lending

Problem: You need a business loan, but your business is either too new or too risky for a conventional bank to put a large sum of money at your disposal.

Solution: Go online and check out peer-to-peer lending. Rather than a single entity putting up a large sum of money, you will be looking at a lot of people chipping in small sums that add up to the total of your loan request.

Here's how it works: You list your loan request on a site like LendingClub.com or Prosper.com and then anyone on the site can see your request and decide if they want to lend you money. This could be your sister, your aunt, or, more likely, a complete stranger who likes what you're planning to do and is looking to lend some money as an investment.

Case study: John Good, the owner of Bubbles Galore Car & Dog Wash in Davison, Michigan, had an idea a few years ago to add a self-serve dog wash to his car wash. He thought this combination would really set him apart from other car washes and that it would make his small business more of a destination than a dreaded chore. He did some market research, looked at trends in the pet industry, and decided it had a reasonable chance for success. All he needed was $16,000 to get it going.

He went back to his bank, which gave him the original mortgage on the car wash, but they refused even to consider a loan for this purpose. That's when John went to "plan B." He listed his business idea and his loan request with LendingClub.com. In less than two weeks, about two hundred people had pitched in to make up his $16,000. The money was instantly deposited in John's account and the payments are automatically taken out every month. The term is three years.

Not every loan listed on peer-to-peer lending sites gets funded. John says he believes he got funded because of a combination of it being a good investment and because he told a good story in the application—which all potential lenders can read. He explained his idea, talked about his research, and was honest about the challenges. In addition, he was a little funny where it was warranted, making him likable. In the end, with peer-to-peer lending, people are lending to other people. Tell a good story and get them interested and you'll have a better chance of getting that loan.

Please note: Not everyone can put up a loan request on these sites. There are strict credit standards and the loans generally top out around $25,000. Interest rates depend on your credit score.

TIP #7
Barter, don't buy

When money is tight, you might be able to hold on to more of it if you can barter goods and services rather than use cash to pay for the things you need.

An easy first step is to approach your lawyer, your accountant, your landlord, and any others who might be willing to trade their services for your product. Reaching out a little farther, you can approach other businesses in your area that sell the supplies or services you need.

Getting even more creative, one business told us they traded the labor of an employee who had a special skill, in this case web design, in exchange for the labor of another company's employee who was great at proofreading. This saved both companies the cost of hiring a freelancer or a contractor to do that extra job.

Finally, there are online barter exchanges where businesses list their offerings and the services they're seeking, hoping to strike a deal to get what they need without paying cash.

Watch out! The IRS has rules about these kinds of barter exchanges, so it's very important to check the regulations that may apply before diving in all the way.

Scan to see a video

TIP #8
Ask your suppliers for funds

You may not realize it, but your suppliers may be willing to lend you funds. After all they have a vested interest in your staying afloat.

New York–based designer (and former Wall Street financial consultant) Aysha Saeed says you should make a list of the companies you buy supplies or services from to run your business. These companies will benefit directly from your success, so why not share your vision and business plan with them? Ask them if they are interested in making a direct investment in your business or if they can give you a line of credit. Aysha recently asked her factory for a $100,000 line of credit and got it. She'll pay it back in one year and her cash flow problems are solved. The factory granted the line of credit because in the long run, her success means more business for them.

Scan to see a video

TIP #9
Ask your customers for payment up front

One way to raise cash quickly is to turn directly to your customers or clients.

By offering a big discount to people who pay in advance for products or services they expect to buy later, you may be able to get the money you need now in a pinch. If you have loyal customers, it may also make sense to let them know why you're doing this. Customers often want to help out a business they're happy with—especially if they're saving money in the process.

Case study 1: In Menlo Park, California, Kepler's Books was just another statistic, another bookstore going under in 2005 in the face of stiff competition from Amazon.com and Barnes & Noble. Unwilling to lose their neighborhood bookstore, a group of committed local customers banded together to help reopen it. They created a "membership plan" where people paid up front to become a Kepler's member and get discounts on future purchases. For instance, the basic membership costs fifty dollars and buys the customer a member rewards card where they get a ten-dollar store credit for every hundred dollars spent. It also gives people a onetime 15 percent–off shopping spree, as well as invitations to "members-only events." This offering raised enough money to keep the store afloat long enough to allow it to enact other key changes to its business model that made it viable once again.

Case study 2: In Hastings-on-Hudson, New York, the owner of a restaurant called Comfort ran into difficulties during the past recession and needed money to pay off the cost of some renovations. The banks were not responsive, so the owner turned directly to his customers for help. He let them know he was struggling and basically asked them for an advance. He offered to sell them VIP cards for $500 each that would have a face value of $600. So right off the bat they got a 20 percent discount by using the cards. Doing this raised nearly $40,000 up front with no strings attached, no monthly payments, and no interest fees. Meanwhile, honoring the cash value of the cards required only the cost of the food, labor, and rent. And there was an added benefit—he created a core group of customers who had a very real interest ($500 worth!) in making sure that restaurant stayed open!

Kepler's

Comfort

Scan to see a video

Scan to see a video

TIP #10
Have a bank loan application strategy

Applying for a loan with too many banks can inadvertently work against you.

Too many bank loan applications can bring down your overall credit score by 5 to 10 points each time your credit gets pulled. That means hitting just five banks for a loan can lower your score by up to 50 points.

Monica Mehta, the managing principal of New York–based investment firm Seventh Capital, suggests you start by applying to those banks that know your business and have experience lending in your industry or in your geographic location. Going to the wrong lenders first may cost you more than you realize.

TIP #11
Find a market for the stuff you're throwing out

Look carefully, there might be a hidden revenue stream being thrown out with the trash! No matter what business you're in, you're likely to be creating waste of some sort—from food scraps to shredded paper to who knows what! It might be worth it to find out if there is a commercial use for this trash.

How do you find out? It's simple. First, figure out what kind of stuff you are throwing out. Then do an Internet search to see what uses there might be for this material. Contact the folks who use it and find out how to sell it to them. The rest is money in the bank.

Case study: Valerio Vindici and Tony DeFilippis are co-owners of Imperial Billiards in New Jersey, a company that makes custom billiard tables. One of their customers noticed all the sawdust lying around their workshop and suggested that they use it to make wood pellets. It didn't take long for Valerio and Tony to find out that wood pellets are pieces of compressed sawdust that are used to fuel pellet stoves, which some homeowners use to heat their homes.

Today these pellets account for 40 percent of the company's sales and have become a steady source of revenue.

Scan to see a video

TIP #12
Be ready with a photo pitch on your phone

Have your cell phone loaded with photos to help you with an impromptu presentation. Gayla Bentley of Houston, Texas, knows a thing or two about successful pitching. She got Barbara Corcoran and Daymond John interested in her plus-size clothing line on the show *Shark Tank*. Gayla's tip is simple: You never know when or where you'll encounter someone interested in your business. Make sure you have an easily accessible link on your smartphone with photos of your product, service, or website so you can show that person a great visual of your business in seconds. On a plane, in a taxi, at a networking event—you always carry your phone; why not make it an easy elevator-pitch accessory? Makes perfect sense to us!

Scan to see a video

CHAPTER TWO

GETTING IT OFF THE GROUND

Launching a new company, product, or service

TIP #13 Focus on the "why"   21

TIP #14 Get fresh ideas from your team's
         brainstorming meeting   23

TIP #15 Make sure you own your material   25

TIP #16 Test your product idea with your
         audience before actually developing it   26

TIP #17 Never do a fifty-fifty partnership   27

TIP #18 Create a buy-sell agreement with
         your partner   28

TIP #19 Ensure that the principals work on
         your account   30

TIP #20 Clear your brand before launching it   31

TIP #21 Get inspired by other industries   33

TIP #22 Give your ideas a name so everyone
         remembers them   34

TIP #23 Internally crowdsource new designs   35

TIP #24 Three key questions to ask in a
         focus group   37

TIP #25 Open up your brainstorming meetings   39

TIP #26 How to compare vendors   41

TIP #13
Focus on the "why"

When you want people to get excited about your company—whether it's an investor, a potential partner, a customer, or even your employees—you need to explain exactly *what* your company does, but you should really focus your presentation on *why* your company does it.

Why? Because people can become inspired by your passion for the work you do even if they're not particularly inspired by the work itself. Focusing on that passion, the "why," won't stop you from talking about what you do, but it will establish a context of why your work is important to you and therefore why it should be important to them as well.

Simon Sinek, the author of *Start with Why: How Great Leaders Inspire Everyone to Take Action,* introduced me to this idea early on in the life of *Your Business* and I have since repeated it to so many others. Simon's theory is that while people may start working with you because of "what" you do, they'll stay loyal to your company because of your vision—"why" you do it. So don't be tempted to spend your time talking about "what" when you'll have much more impact if you focus on the "why."

How I use this: Simon sat down with me to illustrate what he meant. He asked me about the "why" behind GoodSearch and I told him, "We are an online shopping mall and Yahoo-powered search engine that donates about a penny per search and a percentage of each purchase to the charity or school of the user's choice." Simon looked at me and I immediately knew I had said the wrong thing.

He then asked me a series of questions including: Do I like working with my brother as a co-founder? What did I do as a hobby when I was in high school? How do I spend my weekends? Admittedly the session felt more like therapy than a business meeting. But in the end, we had found my "why."

I believe that the opportunity to do good should exist every day and not just when we write a check to our favorite charity. GoodSearch gives people the ability to do good in their everyday lives. It is this "why"—the reason we started GoodSearch—that is helping it to become a transformational new approach to philanthropy. At the end of my conversation with Simon, it was clear that the "why" of my company is much more magnetic than the "what." And once you hook them with the "why," the "what" is easy!

TIP #14
Get fresh ideas from your team's brainstorming meeting

Make sure you get input from everyone at your brainstorming sessions. The theory behind brainstorming is that people in a group are more likely to come up with creative ideas than they would if they were working alone. Well, that might be fine in theory, but in reality many of your best people might not be so good in groups. Often, teams are dominated by a few highly outgoing types who control the conversation while the shy, more reflective types never have their voices heard.

If you're really looking for a fresh perspective, it's the quiet ones you'll want to hear from. That can be hard when they usually get shut out of the conversation. Here's how you can be sure to get everyone's input.

Before calling your staff in for a brainstorming session, send an e-mail around to everyone who's invited. Let them know exactly the topic you will be tackling in the meeting. This gives all the participants some time to come up with good ideas before even walking through the door. Then, during the meeting, you can go around the room one by one and be sure that everyone has the time to offer something. As is the nature of brainstorms, those good ideas will then spark the group to generate even better ideas.

How I use this: We always ask everyone to come into brainstorming meetings with three ideas on a particular topic. Since we started doing this, the ideas that have come out of the meetings have been much more creative. Why? Well, let's face it. Our entire staff is incredibly busy, and in the past when we'd call a meeting, chances are some people didn't even take three minutes to think about the discussion topic ahead of time. As a result, the meetings were slower to take off and people were a little less engaged. Now, with the three-idea rule, everyone's excited to share their ideas, since they've take the time to come up with them, and the brainstorms are much more productive.

TIP #15
Make sure you own your material

If you hire a consultant or contractor to do work for you, as a general rule anything they invent or create will belong to them unless you have made a contractual agreement in advance. For example, if you get someone to write a piece of software, even though it was for your company, the contractor may own the software and be able to do with it what he or she wants—even give it to your competitor! The same goes for design.

Intellectual-property lawyer David Weiss, of Knobbe, Martens, Olson & Bear, says you should consider this issue during the hiring process. You may have to pay more to get the rights assigned to you, but depending on what you're having done, it may well be worth it!

Please keep in mind that having a "work for hire" provision in your agreement may not be enough to cover this. Your agreement should include a "fall back" clause that states that in the event any copyrightable material does not qualify as a "work made for hire," the material is assigned to you. The agreement should further explicitly assign other types of intellectual property to you, such as inventions, trade secrets, etc.

Be careful: Marianne Carlson, otherwise known as "Your Granny Geek," says that if you hire a developer to create your website, make sure you own your domain name, not them! Often, web designers purchase the domain names in their own names. This means that they can restrict your access to your own site.

TIP #16
Test your product idea with your audience before actually developing it

Problem: You have an idea for a new product or service but aren't sure if your customers will be interested in it.

Solution: Put the idea out there and see how many people sign up for it—even *before* the product or service exists! Here's the thing—if you simply put up a survey asking people if they would be interested in your new service, chances are a lot of people are going to say yes because they like you and /or the service you currently provide. But how many of those yeses will actually turn into sales? It's hard to guess.

You don't have to. Let your customers know that you have XYZ product available and that they should sign up for it if they are interested (do *not* let them know that this is simply market research). The number of responses you get will give you a clear indication of interest. If you decide to go ahead with the product, you can let the people who expressed interest know that it's coming soon. If you decide not to, you can let those same people know that you have decided not to go ahead with your plans. Since they dedicated neither time nor money to this, you will most likely not make anyone upset with this change.

Case study: Silvia Dontcheva, who runs Uptown Soap Co. in New York, makes gift soaps, lotions, candles, and solid perfumes. Each time she comes up with a new product, she creates a digital image of what it will look like and offers it to her clients. If they love it, she goes into production. If nobody's interested, she's spent nothing on giving it a try!

TIP #17
Never do a fifty-fifty partnership

Don't set yourself up for a painful standoff. A fifty-fifty partnership has a nice ring to it when you're first starting up a company. All for one and one for all. Unfortunately, as the company grows and the valuation increases, this kind of structure can bring important decision making to a dead halt.

When Gary Erickson started up his company Clif Bar & Company in 1992, it was a small project fueled by little more than his excitement for creating what he thought was the first good-tasting energy bar and sharing it with his buddies. Back then, he says he didn't bother with legal advice, and in the long run he paid a very high price. When the two co-owners received a buy-out offer of $120 million, Gary's partner wanted to take the offer but Gary did not.

The fifty-fifty partnership created an impasse that wasn't resolved until Gary agreed to pay his partner her share of what they would have received from the buyer if they'd sold the company. Gary doesn't regret keeping the company, but he says he should have been more careful when he set up his partnership and that he should have kept a majority interest for himself. If he'd done that, he says he'd have saved himself millions of dollars and a ton of stress.

Scan to see a video

TIP #18
Create a buy-sell agreement with your partner

Don't enter a partnership without a solid exit strategy. When you enter into a partnership with someone to start a business, it's hopefully because you trust and like that person. But can you say the same for their spouse?

From day one of your partnership, create a buy-sell agreement, which spells out what happens in the event of the death, disability, or retirement of one of the partners/owners. The surviving partners will most likely want to continue running the company without having to answer to the departing partner's beneficiaries (such as their spouse or children).

You'll need to get a lawyer to write up this agreement (or if you want to spend a little less money, you can go to a site like RocketLawyer.com or LegalZoom.com). In order to prepare yourself, Leslie Thompson, managing principal of Spectrum Management Group in Indianapolis, says these are the key things to think about:

• How are you going to value your business at the time of this event? Deciding on that methodology ahead of time reduces the chances that you'll be fighting over valuation numbers down the road.

• What are the events that will trigger the buy-sell agreement? Death and disability are the most typical, but other reasons include bankruptcy, divorce, retirement, or a general desire to sell an individual's interest.

• How is the purchase going to be funded to not compromise the liquidity needs of the business? In the case of death or disability, the use of life and disability insurance to fund the buyout is the most common. In the event of retirement or an owner's desire to sell, it's common to provide a structured buyout over a period of several years.

Determining your company's value: Valuing a private business is a tricky thing to do. If both sides cannot decide on a formula, here's another thing you can try. Agree upon a process whereby if, at the time of the trigger, you cannot agree on a price, you hire an appraiser. If both sides don't agree with the appraiser's value, each party can pick their own appraiser and those two appraisers can then pick a third appraiser. From that point on, either the third appraiser can be the deciding appraiser or it could be an average of the three of them. Yes, it's complicated, but it keeps it fair and in the hands of people who are objective.

Important note: Your buy-sell agreement should be reviewed from time to time—at least once every five years.

TIP #19
Ensure that the principals work on your account

Problem: When you are pitched by a public relations company, or another service business, you'll get the full-court press—lunch, senior executives, and a lot of promises. Then, later on, when you've signed up for their service, you may never see those senior executives again. Instead you get lower-level, less-experienced associates working on your projects.

Solution: Ivy Cohen, founder of Ivy Cohen Corporate Communications in New York, says be careful. You have to ensure right from the start that the senior professionals who make the pitch for your business are going to stay engaged on your account once you choose to hire their firm. And the only way to do this is to put it in writing in the contract.

Keep in mind, it's typical to have a lower-level account executive be your day-to-day contact. That said, you should make it contractually clear how often the senior staff will get involved with your account. This could range from having someone senior on your monthly or weekly status-report calls to having them attend a business review every quarter.

If you talk about this (and put it in the contract) right from the start, everyone's expectations will be clear and you'll minimize the risk of any misunderstandings.

TIP #20
Clear your brand before launching it

Before you launch any brand, make sure you are not violating anybody's trademark!

Gadi Navon, a lawyer at Los Angeles–based Strategic Law Partners, LLP, often advises small businesses on intellectual-property matters. He says that he cannot count the number of times he's seen a company invest extraordinary amounts of time and money in developing a brand only to receive a cease and desist letter soon after launch saying they're in violation of someone else's trademark. By "brand" Gadi is not just referring to the name of your company—it means the name or trademark that you use to market your product or service.

Doing your due diligence on this is relatively easy. Start off by doing a simple Internet search. You should also do a word search at the United States Patent and Trademark Office (USPTO—www.uspto.gov).

If you don't see your brand there, though, you're still not quite in the clear. In the United States, companies receive certain trademark rights simply by use. So, even if someone has not bothered to register their brand as a trademark, if they've been using it, you could be in violation of their rights if you use the same or confusingly similar name for similar products or services. The best way to check this is to hire a company that specializes in trademark searches. This issue is complex, so it makes sense to hire a lawyer to help you analyze the reports and advise you on how you should proceed with your proposed brand.

Protecting your own brand: Once you have cleared your brand, you should take your own measures to protect it. For example, you should consider filing an application with the USPTO for registration of the trademark. Also, to put the public on notice that you are claiming the brand as a trademark, you should use the ™ symbol to designate it as a trademark, and if you actually get your trademark registered, you can use the ® symbol for the same purpose. (Note: You cannot use the ® symbol unless you have obtained registration from the USPTO for your trademark.)

TIP #21
Get inspired by other industries

Look beyond your industry to find inspiration to make your product stand out. If you want to distinguish yourself from the crowd and competition, you don't want to look like everyone else.

Case study: Steven Smith, who is based in Portland, Oregon, and is the founder of Stash Tea and Tazo Tea (both of which he sold) and the current owner of Steven Smith Teamaker, was trying to come up with a new design for his packaging. Instead of looking at what other tea companies were doing, he spent some time looking at products from industries completely unrelated to his. He ended up using perfume box and stationery box designs as inspirations rather than traditional tea box designs. And, it worked. His boxes of tea look nothing like the rest of the boxes in his category, and as a result, they really stand out on the store shelves!

Scan to see a video

TIP #22
Give your ideas a name so everyone remembers them

Problem: You've explained a good idea to your team, who all seem to be receptive to it. At the next meeting, however, everyone has already forgotten about it.

Solution: Give all of your projects clever names that people will not forget.

Case study: Brian Hecht, the former CEO of Kikucall (which he has since sold), came up with a big transformational idea to acquire new customers. He ran it by his team and they were all excited. One week later, when he started talking about the big plan at a staff meeting, nobody knew what he was talking about. He tried to explain the idea again, but it came out a little fuzzy. He suddenly realized if he couldn't rally his team and get them to focus on this initiative, it would be dead in the water—even though everyone loved it initially.

He thought about the problem and distilled it down to one simple issue: He needed to take something that was still in the idea stage and make it memorable and concrete. So he gave it a name: "Operation Gargoyle"—a name so intentionally strange that no one would ever forget it. He didn't make an announcement; he simply started referring to it that way. Before he knew it, others were talking about Operation Gargoyle, and magically things started getting done.

TIP #23
Internally crowdsource new designs

Figuring out how to test any new design or redesign is always a challenge. If you leave it to just one person—even a professional—you might end up with a botched project. Instead, take advantage of all of the brain power in your office and crowdsource.

Case study: Ian Aronovich of GovernmentAuctions in Great Neck, New York, says that when designing a new website, logo, or anything creative in nature, every person in the office gets involved in giving him feedback. Here's how he does it to keep things efficient:

First, he sends out the design via e-mail and asks everyone to send back as many comments as they have with a minimum of two.

The design team then goes over these comments and incorporates as many ideas as they feel make sense.

Next, Ian sends out the latest version and asks the team for a maximum of three comments. The design team once again incorporates these notes into the next version.

When this next design goes out to the staff, Ian now asks everyone to send in only their most important comment.

Once the design team finishes incorporating the last round of comments, Ian holds an open forum over lunch or drinks where everyone can just shout out any ideas or changes that have not been integrated. As the CEO, he jots them all down, decides what he thinks is relevant, and relays it back to the design team.

Watch out! By putting designs out to everyone, you might have to sort through comments that are off the wall or take a concept in another direction. Crowdsourcing can be a great tool for generating ideas, but it can also be time-consuming to sort through and carefully consider all of them.

TIP #24
Three key questions to ask in a focus group

It's always helpful to get feedback in order to keep your company focused and relevant. One way to do this is to hold an informal focus group among your employees, customers, or target market.

If you want to get the most useful information, it's best to ask open-ended questions—questions that can't be answered with a simple yes or no. Also bear in mind that negative answers can be just as productive as positive answers, as long as you follow up each response with lots of how's and why's. Clay Dethloff, formerly of Harris Interactive, says there are three basic questions to include:

- "What comes to mind when you think of... (our menu, the competition, the neighborhood, etc.)?" A good way to start out is to get a very general opinion. Asked this way, the answer can go in many directions that you may not have expected. From there you can narrow your focus with the next question.

- "Tell me what you like (don't like) about... (a specific item on the menu, prices charged by the competition, parking in the neighborhood, etc.)." Again this is not a simple yes-or-no question. It forces the speaker to come up with a full answer and often it will include information you didn't think about or know.

- "On a scale of 1–10 (good to bad), what do you think about... (a specific item on the menu, prices charged by the competition, parking in the neighborhood, etc.)." This requires them to put a stake in the ground about their views. Once they've answered, you need to follow up with a lot of specific questions about how they got to that number, what it would take to make the number higher or lower, etc.

TIP #25
Open up your brainstorming meetings

Do not underestimate your staff's ability to think beyond their job title and responsibilities.

Generally when companies have marketing meetings, they invite the marketing staff; with PR meetings, they invite the PR staff...you get the picture. But once in a while, in these targeted meetings, it's worth inviting people from *different* departments. Often that's where your fresh ideas will come from. At GoodSearch, we've developed some wonderful marketing ideas that originated from a person on our tech team. The truth is, if he were relegated to only programming the site, we'd have missed out on a lot of really great contributions.

Case study: Dan Martin, CEO of IFX Forum, Inc., in San Diego, says that, as a business owner, his first instinct is to want his employees to be productive at all times and to not waste time in meetings. However, he came to the realization that sometimes gathering everyone together can be incredibly beneficial.

One of the markets IFX serves is the franchise industry. As a way to increase his company's value to this industry, Dan brought together his product team to brainstorm a new application to increase communication between franchisors and franchisees. They batted around a bunch of ideas, but kept hitting a wall. So Dan did something he doesn't usually do—he called in the entire IFX staff and presented them with the issue. This included everyone—the receptionists, account managers, marketers, and developers—including a number of people he would not have expected to have a solution to the problem. Within minutes, someone at this second meeting suggested creating a video channel for the clients. It clicked with everyone immediately, and the company implemented the idea. Today, that video application remains one of their most well-received products.

TIP #26
How to compare vendors

When comparing vendors to provide your company with a service, be up front about the fact that you are shopping around and then ask for their help in making the decision. While you do not want to put your vendors in the position of having to put each other down, you can ask for specific items that they would suggest you ask their competitors in order to make a fair comparison.

How I use this: When I decided to outsource the HR functions for GoodSearch, I spoke to two professional employer organizations (PEOs) to get their proposals. Before going into the final presentations, I said to each of them that I wanted to make sure I was comparing "apples to apples" and asked if there was anything that might sound the same to someone from the outside (me) but that was in reality quite different about the services they provided.

Through their answers, I was clued in to questions that I otherwise would not have known to ask. For example, one of them said to me, "Ask if the medical rates they give you are good for one year or based on the renewal of their relationship with the provider." It had never occurred to me to ask this before, yet it was an incredibly important point.

Remember, the worry with doing something new is that, generally, you don't know what you don't know. This gives you a way to at least get down to the right questions!

CHAPTER THREE

BEING THE LEADER

Understanding your business and yourself

TIP #27 Make a list of companies that could buy your business · 45

TIP #28 Listen to your lawyers—but always ask questions 46

TIP #29 Manage your advisory board effectively 47

TIP #30 Swap jobs with your business partner 49

TIP #31 Learn to work with your business partner 50

TIP #32 Don't be deceived by paying attention to the wrong numbers 52

TIP #33 Mystery shop your store 54

TIP #34 Be your business's best customer 55

TIP #35 Put yourself in your employees' shoes 56

TIP #36 Keep track of your competitors 58

TIP #37 Treat your suppliers as part of your team 59

TIP #38 Talk to employees of your potential partners, not just management 61

TIP #39 Never be surprised by your cash situation 62

TIP #40 Improve self-confidence by standing differently 63

TIP #41   Do not share your bad mood with
          your staff   65

TIP #42   Knock off unpleasant tasks first thing
          in the morning   66

TIP #43   Ask for your own review   67

TIP #44   Learn from your failures   69

TIP #45   Don't do favors simply to get paid back 70

TIP #46   Pretend you have a boss   71

TIP #27

Make a list of companies that could buy your business

One of the best ways to figure out what your company is good at is to understand why another company would want to acquire you.

Dave Berkus, who is based in Arcadia, California, and one of the most active angel investors in the country, performs one exercise every few years with the boards he sits on: He has them list ten companies that could buy their business.

Here's how he does it:

On a whiteboard, he draws four columns and ten rows. The columns: "Candidate Acquirer," "What They Want," "What We Want," and the "Likelihood" of being acquired:

Candidate Acquirer	What They Want	What We Want	Likelihood (1–10)
Company 1	Our distribution	Their R&D	7
Company 2	Our product	Their money	8
Company 3	Our distribution	Combine ops for cost	6
Company 4	Our distribution	Their money	8

He then has the team brainstorm around these criteria. For the "What They Want" column, the team thinks about what makes them a good acquisition target. For the "What We Want" column, the team focuses on things they are lacking. Dave says the most interesting part of this exercise comes when the team looks at column number two. Generally, at least four of the ten candidates would want the same thing out of an acquisition. Suddenly, it becomes very clear what the company's core competencies are and where its resources should be directed.

TIP #28
Listen to your lawyers—but always ask questions

It's a lawyer's job to point out a risk, but it's your job to assess it. Even if your attorney highlights a potentially terrible downside to a decision you are considering, don't change gears right away without getting more details. That is, you must learn to ask clear and definitive questions so you can form your own opinions and make a sound business judgment.

Case study: Will Dean, the founder of Tough Mudder in Brooklyn, New York, runs a business challenging people to a crazy ten-mile obstacle course. His lawyer warned him that someone they were in a petty dispute with might be able to get an injunction against one of the company's high-profile events. Will pushed back. He asked some shrewd questions about the actual likelihood of really being shut down. By asking the right questions, Will learned that the courts hardly ever issue injunctions and that the standards for getting them to do so are incredibly onerous. Had Will not asked his lawyer these tough questions, he may have made decisions that were bad for business just to avoid something that would likely never happen.

Scan to see a video

TIP #29
Manage your advisory board effectively

Your best resource for advice should be the members of your advisory board—that's why you have them. So how do you keep them engaged in helping your company? Jules Shell, who runs the nonprofit Foundation Rwanda in New York, says it's all about making sure the board members are getting as much out of the experience as you are. Here are some ways she's ensured her board stays involved and excited:

• Choose an interesting group of people with a wide range of skills so that they are able to learn from one another and feel pride in being a part of this group.

• Never be afraid to ask for help. Your board doesn't expect you to know everything, and they want to be a part of the team.

• Have regular and concise communications. Quarterly written e-mails, conference calls, or newsletters help them stay involved.

• Try to convene the entire advisory board face-to-face at least twice a year. You will gain the most by having everyone in one room together. And, back to point number one, if they feel like they're gaining some insight from one another, they'll look forward to the meetings too.

• Finally, set expectations right from the start. Make very clear what you expect of your board members and what they should expect from you. Do you want someone you can call at three a.m.? Tell them that from the start. Do you only need someone to be at the board meeting? Make that clear so they don't think their involvement will be too time-consuming! You do not want one of your board members to become annoyed a few months in because you are asking too much or too little of them.

TIP #30
Swap jobs with your business partner

Problem: Your team is burned out and you've all hit a plateau at work. You need some fresh ideas, but don't have the money to hire anyone new.

Solution: As Ben Tsen, managing director of TZG Partners in Shanghai, China, explains it, "Switch jockeys in the middle of the race." He says that when you get to the point where the doldrums set in, consider doing the unthinkable—switch seats with your partner or a senior member of your team. You take on his/her role and vice versa (if not for every task, then at least for a portion of them). Since you have been working together for a while, the handover process should be relatively smooth. What you'll find is that this is a very low-risk and low-cost way of getting new blood and new energy into the company, and does wonders for everybody's motivation, momentum, and creativity.

TIP #31
Learn to work with your business partner

The relationship you have with your business partner can be one of the most important relationships you have in your life—and it's certainly critical to the success of your company. Julie Hermelin and Paulette Light, founders of Friendex, in Los Angeles, say these are the keys to maintaining a good relationship:

• Have a clear conversation before partnering and then periodically touch base once the company launches about each of your strengths and weaknesses. For example, Paulette is more business-minded and Julie is more creative. They joke about how the concept of "morning" to Paulette means eight a.m. whereas to Julie "morning" is any time before noon. Imagine how tension-creating it could be if they didn't call this out ahead of time and they were each expecting something in the "morning."

• If your partner feels really strongly about something and your opinion is opposite but not as strong, give in. If you both feel strongly, fight it out, and listen to each other's reasoning as it affects the big picture of the company and your mutual goals. If you can't agree, be willing to find a solution that's different from what either of you is offering.

• Never give feedback to each other in an e-mail—always do it over the phone or in person. And never give it in a highly emotional tone.

• Be grateful, acknowledge what works, and bring your best self to your interactions. In the same way you let your employees know what they're doing well (see tip #67), make sure you let your partner know too.

Tip: Nina Kaufman, founder of Ask the Business Lawyer, says that when you are thinking of working with a partner, always be sure to exchange your credit information. You'd hate to apply for a loan down the road and be surprised to learn that your partner has poor credit.

TIP #32
Don't be deceived by paying attention to the wrong numbers

While numbers are the lifeblood of any business, not all numbers are equally meaningful. For example, if your shop is full of visitors, that might look great from the street. But if those visitors aren't buying anything, you're in deep trouble.

Eric Ries, Harvard Business School Entrepreneur-in-Residence and bestselling author of *The Lean Startup*, says the numbers you should watch are those that indicate the success of an action you want people to take. For example, if you want people to sign up for a service or buy an item, that's the important number you need to watch and measure.

Here's how it might work. Let's say what's most important to you is how well your retail site is doing in converting visitors into buyers. On an average day, suppose a hundred people come to your site and twenty of them buy something—you'd have a 20 percent conversion rate. Then, one week you do a big advertising campaign and a thousand people come to your site and two hundred of them purchase something. Well, if you just looked at the raw number of people coming to the site or the raw number of people who bought something, that would sure look good. But if you look at that conversion rate, it actually stayed the same—20 percent. So, while you increased visitors and sales through advertising, your advertising did nothing to improve the conversion rate!

So you need to figure out the numbers that truly reflect how your company is doing and then get a report card on those every day, week, or month. Those are the key numbers you need.

How I use this: At GoodSearch, we all look at our relevant numbers right when we walk in the door every morning. This helps Scott Garell, our CEO, understand what's working and what's not. With this information, he knows which levers to push to make sure we're on track to meet our monthly and yearly goals. If something looks a little off, he knows to go have a conversation with the employee who "owns" that part of the business to see if he or anyone else on the team can provide some help. And, on the flip side, if things are ahead of schedule, Scott has the opportunity to give some concrete positive feedback and to think about what else can be done to keep the accelerated momentum. As Scott says, you never want to be surprised at the end of the month or year by numbers that are way off your projections!

TIP #33
Mystery shop your store

It's hard to know how well your staff is treating your customers or clients when you are not around to watch them. One way to keep an eye on your employees is to use mystery shoppers. Judi Hess, from the mystery shopping company Customer Perspectives, gave us some tips on how to make mystery shopping work for your business:

1. Make sure to let your employees know that there will be a mystery shopping customer evaluating them. Don't tell them the exact time or date, of course. Simply let them know you have hired some mystery shoppers. It's always better to be up front. If your staff doesn't know about this, they may feel resentful and spied upon.

2. Remind your employees what is expected of them. That alone can improve their behavior.

3. Share mystery shopping results so your employees can see what they are doing right and wrong. If someone is singled out for something negative, bring it to their attention and ask them what they could have done differently. If the report is good, and everyone performed well, reward them. At LaBonne's Markets, in Connecticut, the reward for a good report is free movie tickets.

Scan to see a video

Note: This isn't only for brick-and-mortar stores. Mystery shoppers can also be used to call the customer service department of your website.

TIP #34
Be your business's best customer

Use your own company's products or services on a regular basis.

Donna Perillo, owner of Sweet Lily Natural Nail Spa & Boutique in New York City, says the best way to determine what your customers' wants and needs are is to be your own customer. "If you own a retail store, shop in it. If it's a restaurant, dine in it. If you make a product, use it. Every week I go to my spa to get some sort of service. I make sure I get the full treatment, have a cup of tea, and listen to the music. It's amazing how differently I see things when I'm in the client seat. I notice if something needs to be cleaned, if the tea is too cold, if the music is too loud. Seeing the store from a customer's perspective helps me make the changes necessary to keep my business from losing its edge."

Tip: Make sure your employees get a chance to use your products and services too.

TIP #35
Put yourself in your employees' shoes

Make time to spend an afternoon doing some of the more mundane work in your company. By seeing things firsthand and joining the people in the tasks they do, you're more likely to pay much more attention the next time they suggest a change or improvement.

How I use this: We have a group of people on our team who are responsible for approving organizations who have applied to be a part of GoodSearch. While I knew the process was somewhat tedious and needed improvement, for me the problem was always a low priority. That is, until I spent an afternoon doing that job! After digging into the task myself for a few hours, I realized how much easier it would be if we just automated part of it. The next day, that improvement went to the top of my to-do list and that whole area of the operation became much more productive.

In truth, you would think this same result could have been accomplished by simply doing a better job of listening to the staff. In this case the woman in charge of that department had actually suggested this change to me several times. And, yes, I did hear her, but since her department was getting the work done, I didn't view her suggestions as a big priority compared with everything else that was going on. Once I put myself in her shoes, however, there was no hiding from it!

More insight: Erik Budde, founder of AboutAirportParking, says that the understanding you get from actually doing a job makes a huge difference when it comes to hiring new employees or finding companies where you can outsource the work.

At his company, Erik makes it a point to answer customer service calls in order to hear firsthand both compliments and complaints. He says that you really need to spend time on the front lines to truly understand what it takes to get the job done.

TIP #36
Keep track of your competitors

Whatever market you're in, you need to be aware of what the other players are doing. If you are not closely watching your competitors, you're missing out on vital information. In a fast-changing marketplace, you can easily lose your foothold if you don't know what moves the other players are making.

The problem is, most small business owners are so swamped with their own business that they don't have time to stay on top of the competition. Matthew Weiss, partner at the law firms Weiss & Associates and 888-Red-Light in New York City, says that there is an easy way to keep up:

• Set up a Google Alert (www.google.com/alerts) and type in the company names that you want to follow—you will then get a daily or weekly e-mail letting you know of all the news and blog mentions for that company.

• While you're at it, add your own company. If someone is talking about your business, you want to know what they are saying.

• Subscribe to competitor newsletters and follow them on Facebook and Twitter.

• Use your competitors' products and services (be a customer) every once in a while.

Michael Port, author of *Book Yourself Solid*, says that if you're going to do this, though, use an alias—set up an e-mail account under a different name. Keep in mind, by the way, that your competitors are probably doing the same to you!

Watch out! Following your competitors too closely can drive you nuts. Keep some perspective and don't change your business model every time you see someone else come up with something new.

TIP #37
Treat your suppliers as part of your team

Your suppliers are critical to your business, so treat them that way.

Case study 1: Since the beginning of his company, Jim McCann, founder of 1-800-Flowers, has invited his suppliers to participate in his highly confidential company meetings. As a result, they are fully aware of the company's projections and are able to scale up efficiently to meet those needs. At the same time, 1-800-Flowers planners can get useful feedback early in the planning stages from those same suppliers. Because the suppliers are brought in early in the process, they can offer suggestions for the most cost-efficient ways to accomplish the company's goals.

While some people may find it a little nerve-racking to share some types of confidential information with outsiders, Jim believes that his core suppliers are as critical to his business as his own employees. As a result, he treats them like they are part of his company.

Case study 2: At Amy's Kitchen in California, the founders, Rachel and Andy Berliner, take a similar approach. They say that early on, instead of going to large suppliers, they went to smaller ones for whom they'd be a more important part of the business. Then they helped these suppliers by signing rock-solid multiyear contracts. With these contracts in hand, the suppliers were able to get the financing they needed to meet the Berliners' expectations. Amy's Kitchen ended up with a solid supply chain of products and services that guaranteed they would be able to deliver on their contracts to their distributors.

In both of these cases, the suppliers who once were small grew as the companies themselves grew. Because of this, they now have incredibly strong relationships and can count on one another in a pinch.

Jim McCann

Scan to see a video

Amy's Kitchen

Scan to see a video

TIP #38
Talk to employees of your potential partners,
not just management

Rachel Weeks, founder of School House in Durham, North Carolina, says that before you enter into any long-term partnership with another company, don't just talk to management, talk to the employees.

When she went around to find a factory to manufacture her high-end collegiate apparel, she spent a lot of time chatting with the factory workers to see if they liked their jobs and, if so, what they liked about them. As her COO, Susan Williams, said, "You know the old saying that the secretary knows it all in an office building? It's true in a factory that the operator knows all as well."

Scan to see a video

TIP #39
Never be surprised by your cash situation

Just because your company is doing well doesn't mean you have enough cash on hand to sustain it. As many guests on our show have told us (particularly those who have advice on how to survive in a rough economy), "Cash is king."

So how do you get a firm and lasting grip on your cash situation? Jim Blasingame, small business expert and award-winning host of *The Small Business Advocate* show, offers this advice:

First, build a twelve-month cash flow spreadsheet in a program such as Excel so you can project and track the monthly relationship between cash collections and cash disbursements from all sources. This planning tool will provide a rolling picture of cash flow in any given month.

Next, look at the "Ending cash" number at the bottom of each month's column. A negative number in any month means you'll need to add cash from sales, reduce expenses, add cash from another source (such as a bank loan), or some combination of the three.

Jim says a banker once told him that if he could bring him only one financial document for a loan request, it should be a twelve-month cash flow projection that includes both how the borrowed cash would be used and the cash flow with the debt service. As Jim says, he always listens to his banker, and so should you!

By the way, once you build this important cash flow spreadsheet, it should become one of your most critical operating tools. This is something you need to update and evaluate monthly. You never want to be surprised that you don't have enough cash on hand to pay the bills! In addition, this will give you a heads-up if you're going to be moving into a tight stretch so you can come up with some solutions in advance.

TIP #40
Improve self-confidence by standing differently

Problem: You're about to attend a high-pressure meeting or make an important presentation. There are a lot of touchy issues—and a tough audience. You need to be calm and confident and you are feeling anything but....

Solution: Prepare for your presentation by spending five minutes before the meeting standing in certain positions and moving your body in certain simple exercises.

Yes, we get it, to many of you, this sounds ridiculous. How could holding your body in certain poses help make you more confident? Well, it does. Amy Cuddy at Harvard Business School and Dana Carney at the University of California, Berkeley, have studied this extensively and they found that positioning yourself in specific ways releases testosterone into your body (for both men and women) which in turn makes you more confident. Their tests also show that the stances they describe lower the level of cortisol in your system, which reduces stress.

So here are some exercises to do before going into an important meeting.

FRANK SILVERSTEIN

- Stand in a pose that "takes up a lot of space" with your legs spread and with your arms out wide.

- Sit with your hands behind your head and your legs up on the desk "CEO style."

FRANK SILVERSTEIN

Amy told us that you should also resist the urge to do what you'd normally do before a stressful meeting: hunch over your cell phone while you're sitting in the waiting room. If you do that, you lower your testosterone and increase your cortisol, which increases stress—the exact opposite of what you want!

Tip: To see Amy teaching me these and other poses, click on the QR code.

Scan to see a video

TIP #41
Do not share your bad mood with your staff

When you're in a bad mood, smile. That's it. Just smile. There is evidence that the simple act of smiling puts you in a better mood. Try it.

Why? As the boss, you simply cannot share your bad mood with your staff. Your employees will definitely feed off the way you feel, and your dark mood will change the whole tenor of the office. If you start complaining or being negative, the culture of the office will quickly become negative.

Bottom line: You set the example for what kind of attitude is OK. If you are grumpy and mean, you're giving other people license to behave the same way.

TIP #42
Knock off unpleasant tasks first thing in the morning

Get difficult or unpleasant tasks done early in the morning. This will relieve much of the anticipated tension of the workday and will help you focus on everything else you have to do later. Even if the results aren't good, at least you'll be able to be proactive and move on to the next step instead of having the task hanging over you all day.

Case study: The day Lisa Everson went to interview Scott Griffith, the CEO of the popular car-sharing company Zipcar, in his office in Cambridge, Massachusetts, she could tell something was on his mind. It was early in the morning and as she was setting up for the interview, he was preoccupied. After a few minutes of banter, he looked at his watch and excused himself to make a phone call. When he came back out for his interview a few minutes later, he was noticeably more relaxed and ready to roll. It made sense, then, that one of his tips for our audience was: "Make tough phone calls in the morning so that you can face the rest of the day and not worry about that hard call."

How I use this: Just recently, I pressed "snooze" about ten times on my Outlook-calendar reminder that I had to "Call landlord to discuss office lease." Instead of making that call in the morning, I found fifty-five reasons why it was very important to clean my desk—and the cabinets near it—and talk to my employees about how we should decorate the new office. In other words, I was creating mindless work for myself in order to procrastinate making that important, though difficult, call. And in the end, the day was somewhat wasted. When I finally did call the landlord, everything worked out and I wished that I had done it earlier so it had not been weighing on me all day.

TIP #43
Ask for your own review

If you want to do better at being the boss, the best people to ask are the ones who are watching your every move—your employees.

Rob Kaplan, a professor of management practice at Harvard Business School and author of the book *What to Ask the Person in the Mirror*, says that because your employees will likely be a little wary of criticizing you, you have to be deliberate in the way you ask for this feedback. First, make a list of the people in your office from whom you'd like to solicit input on your strengths and weaknesses. Then, meet with each of these people individually and explain that you need their help. Ask them each to give you advice on one or two tasks or skills they believe you could improve on.

Keep in mind, your employees are going to be nervous about doing this and chances are they'll say, "I can't think of anything," or you're going to have to wait through a pregnant pause as they figure out what they can and cannot say. You should patiently say to them that you really want one specific suggestion and that it would really help you. It's up to you to make them feel comfortable and understand that they should speak freely. They will carefully watch to see how you react when they speak, so show them that you are sincere and really interested. After the meeting, show them that you are taking their feedback seriously and acting on what they shared with you.

By the way, when you hear what your employees have to say, chances are it'll be like a shot in the heart and a little devastating, primarily because you'll know it's true. The key to making this work is, of course, to be open and not defensive. True, it might be a little painful, but in the long run, if you truly listen and act on their suggestions, you'll become that much more effective as a leader.

Scan to see a video

TIP #44
Learn from your failures

When you fail at something, instead of giving up, just try it again but in a different way—or at least identify what went wrong so you don't repeat it.

My mother used to tell me that when something goes awry, take ten minutes or an hour to cry about it and then move on. New York–based high-net-worth advisor Lewis Schiff told me about the research he's done to find out what makes people successful. It sounded very familiar when he said that successful people do not wallow in their failures.

Lewis says "failure" is all just a state of mind. When something goes wrong, do not spend your time blaming others or feeling shamed. Instead, think of the experience as a teaching moment. According to Lewis's research, many successful entrepreneurs fail and fail often. But, in the face of failure, they reexamine their own behavior and look at what they could have done differently. And then they try a new approach.

While part of this is personality driven, you can indeed change the way you act by just being aware of it. This can be as simple as sitting down and listing on the left side of a piece of paper all of the things that went wrong with your endeavor. On the right side, list what you wish you had done in retrospect. Then use that list on the right side as a manual for how to act going forward.

Jim Koch, founder of Samuel Adams beer, says that he's experienced a lot of failures in his business in the form of beers they spent time and money on developing that just didn't make it. He admits that it's incredibly disappointing each time. But each time this happens, he sits down with his team and says, "OK, what can we learn from this?"

Scan to see a video

TIP #45
Don't do favors simply to get paid back

Don't think of business favors as things that need to be paid back. Think of them as reputation builders for yourself. The more you help people, the more people will respect you and look to you for leadership, which will in turn help your business.

Alfred Edmond Jr. of *Black Enterprise* and a frequent guest on *Your Business*, said it well: "Not everyone whose back you scratch will be able—or even willing—to scratch yours. Don't worry about that; that's not the point." He says helping others is not about a quid pro quo. It's about being part of a network of successful businesses. Your goal should not be to obligate others to do things for you. It should be to be recognized as a contributor to the success of your circle of business acquaintances. Once that happens, others will want you to succeed too. It's sort of the corporate version of "paying it forward."

As I see it, business is about relationships, and in the best relationships, you do not keep score.

Key thought: Paul Sethi, CEO of Advertising Red Books, echoed this same sentiment, saying you should put yourself out there and expect nothing in return. He says, "Leverage whatever skills you have to help other budding entrepreneurs—and not just friends, but all who show passion, drive, and focus in what they are setting out to create or innovate. Do not set out with any agenda, or expect to be repaid, thanked, or recognized in any way—do it to learn, to mentor and to stay on the edge of innovation yourself."

TIP #46
Pretend you have a boss

One of the tough things about being the boss is that you don't have a boss motivating you to get your work done.

Denise Blasevick, CEO and founding partner of the marketing company the S3 Agency in Boonton, New Jersey, has a great idea to remedy this issue: Pretend you do have a boss. Basically, give yourself a review and then live up to your "boss's" expectations. This little trick will give you immediate clarity regarding your priorities, both long term and short term.

CHAPTER FOUR

CREATING YOUR TEAM

Hiring, firing, evaluating, and other HR issues

TIP #47 Fire quickly   74

TIP #48 Don't give raises during a performance review   76

TIP #49 Tap the business school workforce   77

TIP #50 Make your recommendation and then step aside   79

TIP #51 Interview multiple candidates for each job   80

TIP #52 Hire staff who match your target demographic   81

TIP #53 Speed up your hiring   82

TIP #54 Ask creative interview questions   83

TIP #55 Hire an alternative workforce   84

TIP #56 Share business objectives to fully engage your freelance workers   85

TIP #57 Get tax breaks for new hires   86

TIP #58 Find the perfect intern   87

TIP #59 Roll out the welcome mat for new employees   88

TIP #60 Create a disagreement protocol   89

TIP #61 Have "expectations meetings" with
your employees   90

TIP #62 Keep employee files with detailed
records   92

TIP #63 Don't keep track of employee time off   93

TIP #64 Cash in the credit card points   94

TIP #47
Fire quickly

This is admittedly the easiest piece of advice to give and the hardest to act upon. In a small company, it's usually obvious early on if you've made a hiring mistake. If that happens, immediately fire that employee.

While that may sound harsh, Phil Town, investment advisor and author of *Payback Time*, says it is the right thing to do. You *must* hire only A-caliber people because they will also hire A people. B people will kill you and your company because they are afraid to hire A's so they hire Cs, and pretty soon you have a company that literally doesn't work. So if you find that a recent hire is just not performing at the A level, give them a dose of tough love and let them go. It's the best way for them to move on in their journey of becoming an A in another setting.

The absolute *wrong* thing to do is to give someone too many chances and hope that things will improve. One hiring mistake can be a drain on your resources and affect employee morale across the company. Even though it's incredibly difficult to fire someone, it's better to do it early on before any serious damage is done.

How I used this: A couple of years ago, I hired a woman for an entry-level position at GoodSearch. While she seemed the perfect fit in the interview and my entire team loved her, after about a week, I knew that I had made a mistake. She was not able to do some very basic tasks that the job required. I felt terrible about the idea of firing her (especially since she turned down another job offer to join my company) and I tried everything I could: I gave her more training; I had someone in the office sit with her for a day; I had discussions with her about her process of learning. Nothing worked. So, while my inclination was to keep trying to make this work, after a few weeks I let her go.

I knew this was the right decision. First, because I felt it in my gut. But secondly, and more importantly, my other employees told me that they had spent the last few weeks annoyed that they were picking up the slack for the person who was hired precisely to make their lives easier. This one hire was undermining the culture of openness, hard work, and cooperation that we had spent so much time building. A few weeks later, I got a call from the woman I had fired referring a friend of hers for the job. She told me that it was actually a relief for her to be fired because she knew the position was not for her. She also said she would have kept trying to make it work even though she was unhappy. Clearly this difficult decision of letting her go when I did was right for everyone.

Note this: Barry Moltz says an easy way to know if you should fire someone is to do the "cringe test." If you are cringing every time you write their paycheck, you know it's time to fire them.

And note this: The other side of this coin is "hire slowly." Though you may need someone right away, hiring the right person is incredibly key to the running of your business. For that reason, do not make rash decisions.

TIP #48
Don't give raises during a performance review

A performance review, if done well, gives you a chance to applaud your employees' good work, give them constructive feedback about things they are not doing well, and set goals for the upcoming year. But Scott Glass, founder of Guerin Glass Architects (and my husband), says that everything you say during a review could be rendered useless if you use that same meeting to discuss a salary increase.

Here's why: If the upshot of your review is positive but your employee receives a much smaller raise than they were expecting, you run the risk that they will come away from the meeting thinking that their work is not valued in spite of all the significant praise you just heaped on them.

Conversely, if the review is somewhat negative and you still give them a raise, the employee may think that they're actually doing all right, in spite of the candid talk you just had with them.

Timing: Overall performance reviews should be done once a year (with "check-ins" as needed throughout the year). But the discussions regarding pay raises should be done totally separately and at least two months after the performance review.

TIP #49
Tap the business school workforce

If you have a business school nearby, you have an amazing resource for thoughtful work at the right price—free. For example, Lani Lazzari, the founder of Simple Sugars in Pittsburgh, convinced a group of students in the business program at Duquesne University to write her business plan.

When I was at Stanford Business School, as part of our course work, a group of us wrote a marketing plan for one local small business, did a comprehensive HR study for another, and did a regression analysis for a third. (If you don't know what a regression analysis is, that's exactly why you want to go and get a bunch of business school students working for you!)

Surprisingly, recruiting this kind of help isn't hard. Simply contact professors who teach business classes (you can get their contact information from the school) and let them know about a specific project you need help with. Many professors will be grateful for the opportunity to provide real-life experiences for their students.

Case study: This is not just limited to business plans and marketing plans. Leslie Haywood, founder of Grill Charms by Charmed Life Products in Charleston, South Carolina, has used local schools for a variety of needs for her company. When she needed engineering drawings to send to her manufacturer, she contacted a local technical college and found an instructor and student to help her for free.

When Leslie needed packaging designs done, she called Clemson University, which has one of the best packaging science departments in the country, and her case was selected to be a senior project for one of the classes. Clemson students (under faculty advisement) designed her packaging from top to bottom. They then performed tests to ensure that the packaging was not only aesthetically pleasing but could withstand the rigors of a twenty-eight-day transit via ocean, rail, and truck if needed. Leslie ended up getting tens of thousands of dollars' worth of quality work for absolutely nothing!

Scan to see a video

TIP #50
Make your recommendation and then step aside

Bringing on another partner or hiring a key employee can be tricky if you're the one introducing the candidate and you feel really strongly in favor of that person. What you don't want to do is push someone on your partner only to have it backfire on you if the two of them don't get along.

Case study: Ross Intelisano, partner of the New York law firm Rich, Intelisano & Katz LLP, says that when he wanted to bring in a former colleague as a new partner to his firm, he didn't want to force the idea on his current partner. So here's what he did: Over a period of months, he slowly pitched his old colleague about joining the firm and separately pitched his partner about adding the old colleague as a partner. Next, when the time was right, he took each of them to lunch separately and told them how strongly he felt about a potential partnership of the three of them. Then he stepped aside and said, "You guys take it from here."

From that point on, Ross stayed out of it and let the two of them get to know each other and make their own decisions. While it was tempting to check in with them to counter any issues they may have had about each other, Ross held off from asking questions. The only way he became involved was in making sure the process was moving along—not whether it would have a positive outcome or not.

In the end, the other two decided on their own that it would work out and they now have a healthy, positive, three-person law partnership.

TIP #51
Interview multiple candidates for each job

When hiring, set up interviews with at least three to five people for a position you are trying to fill, even before meeting the first person. Belinda DiGiambattista, the owner of Butter Beans, Inc., in New York, says if you don't schedule multiple interviews in advance, it can be tempting to hire the first person you meet (if they seem qualified). You may not realize at that point there are better candidates out there.

In addition, after comparing several candidates, it will become clear if nobody is the perfect match. Each candidate may have one characteristic that's perfect and you should keep interviewing until you find someone who has it all.

How I use this: At GoodSearch, we also interview each serious candidate in at least three different places, such as our office, a coffeehouse, and on a walk down the street. You learn much more about people when you mix up the location and scenery than you would by having them come to the office multiple times. And at a small business, this is just as important to do for an administrative assistant as a department head, because you will all work very closely together.

TIP #52
Hire staff who match your target demographic

If you have people on your staff who fit the demographic of your target audience, you've got yourself an in-house focus group and an ever-ready guerilla marketing team.

When his company was just starting out, Blake Mycoskie, of TOMS, created a loyalty-inspiring internship program. Every summer he hired about twenty students, who did whatever Blake and his team needed them to do—write copy, deliver shoes, host events, etc. Each of these interns was in the TOMS demographic, so in addition to getting cheap labor for the summer, Blake also had a group of twenty people who were fanatical about the brand and were eager to spread the word to their friends, providing the most effective marketing you could ask for: word of mouth. They also came up with great ideas to help grow the business among their peers.

This is not limited to students. If you're hiring temporary help and the job does not require a specific skill, consider hiring someone in your target demographic. For example, if you're selling diapers, don't necessarily go to the local college to get your summer help; find some local moms who want to work part-time. If you're selling products to baby boomers, recruit retirees, many of whom may be interested in part-time work.

Postscript: Another very smart thing Blake did was to provide room and board for all of his summer interns in one big house for the summer. This created a bond among them that also helped strengthen their loyalty to the brand.

Scan to see a video

TIP #53
Speed up your hiring

Problem: You put out a job listing and got back a blizzard of résumés. It can be tricky and time-consuming to determine who is truly passionate about—and qualified for—the job.

Solution 1: Before she considers any résumé, Camille Gaines, the founder of FinancialWoman in Austin, Texas, responds to every candidate by sending a list of detailed questions about their schedule, availability, skills, and the type of work they most like to do. In addition, she lets them know about her work habits and preferences. This immediately weeds out people who are not suited to the position. If they don't respond, clearly they were not that interested in the job in the first place. If they do respond, she can quickly scan the responses to see if it's worth bringing them in to interview.

Solution 2: Bibby Gignilliat, CEO of Parties That Cook, also asks a number of questions, though she does it right at the "submit your résumé" stage on her website. In the job posting itself, she directs candidates to answer three questions in their cover letter. These differ for each job opening, but an example of what she'd ask someone applying for a marketing job is, "If you could make two recommendations for our website, what would they be?" Many candidates don't notice this request—which automatically highlights their lack of attention to detail and lack of commitment to the process. In this way she easily eliminates the first batch of unsuitable candidates.

TIP #54
Ask creative interview questions

It's hard to really get to know someone in an hour-long interview. So instead of simply asking the old standbys, such as "What are you good at?" and "Why do you want to work here?" ask things that get to the heart of what you're trying to find out. A good interview question also tells your candidate as much about the company as their answer tells you about them.

How I use this: One question I always ask in an interview is "Would you be willing to put together an IKEA bookcase?" When we first started GoodSearch, this was actually a somewhat real question, as we moved offices a lot and had to put together a lot of IKEA bookcases. But even now that we have a long lease and a fully furnished office, I still ask it. Why? First, it gives me a sense of what kind of person I'm speaking with. We're not interested in hiring anyone who feels any task is beneath them, whether it's actually part of their job description or not. Second, and this is equally important, this question sends a message to the candidate that we do not have a hierarchical environment. When something needs to get done, everyone, from the CEO on down, pitches in. If this is not the kind of place the interviewee wants to work, I'll immediately see their enthusiasm for the job begin to wane.

TIP #55
Hire an alternative workforce

Problem: You are looking for a cost-effective way to hire people to assemble, package, and fulfill orders and you don't want to go overseas.

Solution: Tap your local disabled employees workshop.

If you do a quick search online, you'll find a number of resources under "Disabled Employees Workshop." These are generally nonprofit organizations dedicated to giving meaningful work to the mentally and physically disabled. The workshops operate much like any light assembly or service shop and they employ people who are good at completing repetitive tasks like packaging and shipping. In addition, your company gets to do its part in providing work for an underserved community.

Case study: When Peter Dering, CEO of Peak Design in San Francisco, launched the Capture Camera Clip System, it was an instant hit. In less than two months, his company had almost six thousand preorders and was faced with gearing up manufacturing to fulfill them. His product, a quick release clip for SLR cameras, had fifteen components, including the packaging. He decided to ship all the components to his workspace in California for assembly, but he needed affordable help to put it all together.

He tapped the services of the San Francisco nonprofit Disabled Employees Rehabilitation. This got him a good price without having to assemble his product overseas (which he thought would bring him a bunch of headaches), and he felt good about the contribution he was making to the community.

TIP #56
Share business objectives to fully engage your
freelance workers

When you work with contractors or freelancers, be sure that they understand your bigger vision and how their work contributes to it. It's difficult to fully engage in a job if you don't really know why you're doing it. So don't keep them in the dark!

It's very common to only share a piece of your business plan with a contractor but not the whole picture. Rama Katkar, of Hipiti, in San Francisco, says freelancers will likely do a better job if they understand and buy into your company's broader goals. For example, if you hire someone to help you with data entry, show them the finished product that their work will contribute to (presentations, analysis, etc.). They will likely become more enthusiastic and diligent if they understand why their work is important.

Tip: The best testing ground for adding a new full-time employee to your business is trying them out as a freelancer first. By fully engaging them in the culture and objectives of your company, you're more likely to get a better idea of their talents and abilities and whether or not they might be a good fit.

TIP #57
Get tax breaks for new hires

Problem: You need to hire additional staff, but money is tight and you're not sure if you can swing it.

Solution: Check your Small Business Development Center for tax breaks and subsidies for new hires.

Brandon Hinkle, one of the cofounders of Chicago-based plura Financial Solutions, says many states have implemented significant incentives to get unemployed people back into the workforce—and the government is willing to foot a significant part of the salary in many cases.

Simply do a search for a Small Business Development Center (SBDC) in your area. These are not-for-profit organizations working with the Small Business Association (SBA) that help business owners get grants, licenses, financing, etc. They are frequently a forgotten and underutilized resource for small businesses.

Watch out! Once you find a benefit that seems like it may work for your company, read the fine print to be sure that it truly applies to your situation. In addition, double-check to see if there's a time limit for how long the subsidy lasts.

TIP #58
Find the perfect intern

While in theory interns are an amazing resource, as they provide a cheap extra set of hands, in practice they are often more work for a manager than they're worth. In the brief time you have allotted to hiring interns, it's hard to figure out who will be a fast learner and who will be a summer loafer.

After six years of hiring interns, Larry Smith, founder of SMITH Magazine in New York, has developed some rules to make sure he gets summer hires who are truly enthusiastic about working for him:

• Make the interns find you! Larry doesn't advertise on Craigslist and listservs, and he makes the job listing on his site very hard to find. Why? The people who take the time to find him and his company's application form are those individuals who are genuinely excited to work for him.

• Make the intern-application process tricky. Larry created a long application that includes having the interns do some of the things they'd be doing if they got the job. If they can't manage the somewhat complicated application process, chances are they're not going to be a great intern.

• Throw them into the fire. Larry has prospective interns spend a day at the office to see how they like it before they seal the deal. He puts them into a typically intense and insane day. If they look at their watch too much in the hope of escaping, he knows they're not right for the job!

Remember: It's generally illegal to hire an intern without paying them (or giving them school credit). You can read more on the specific rules here: http://www.sba.gov/community.

TIP #59
Roll out the welcome mat for new employees

It doesn't have to be pricey for a small business to make a big impression and welcome a new employee onboard. Dana Hughens of Clairemont Communications in Raleigh, North Carolina, recommends this simple first-day combo:

- Be organized and present the employee handbook with all of the important information, company policies and procedures, contact numbers, and mission statement.

- Also provide less formal details, including the best place to get coffee or snacks along with a gift card to the local hangout so that he or she can check it out and begin to feel part of the group.

- Put a few special goodies, such as office supplies and a flower in a bud vase, on his or her desk to welcome the employee to your company.

How I use this: Since the early days when my first Good-Search employees were working in my one-bedroom apartment, I have always had a company T-shirt, fresh flowers, and all of the employment forms sitting on his or her desk on the first day a new employee starts work. While this may not seem like a big deal, taking the time to do something small shows that you are: (a) organized and (b) happy that the person is joining the team. This goes a long way to making someone feel like they made the right choice in joining your company. Kari, one of our very first employees, told me that seeing the flowers on her desk (aka my dining room table) when she walked in gave her the sense that we truly valued the people who worked with us.

TIP #60
Create a disagreement protocol

Disagreements are bound to happen in almost any office, so prepare for them before they happen with a clear procedure.

Michael Bosma, managing shareholder of the Bosma Group in Reno, Nevada, suggests inserting a disagreement protocol into your employee manual. This way you can spell out how you expect your employees to proceed if they have a disagreement with someone else in the office. Michael says this is the best idea he's ever implemented.

Here's Michael's policy: If someone is on a rant about someone else, they should speak about the problem directly with that person. If someone complains to Michael, the first thing he does is ask if they addressed it directly. This immediately ends the gossip. New members to Michael's team tell him it's the most positive work environment they have encountered.

Watch out! If you implement a policy like this, make sure to allow for exceptions, such as when someone feels uncomfortable speaking directly to the person with whom they have a problem. Your protocol should be flexible enough to also allow people to speak with their managers as necessary.

TIP #61
Have "expectations meetings" with your employees

Once a year, set time aside to have a one-on-one "expectations meeting" with each of your employees.

This is not a review and should not be included in a review. Rather than a place to discuss strengths and weaknesses, it's simply a conversation between you and your employee about what you two should expect out of each other in your working relationship.

Bruce Sellery, founder of Moolala in Calgary, Canada, says that this meeting gives everyone a chance to communicate what they expect of one another, and, even more important, creates a touchstone that both parties can return to when issues arise. So, for example, as the boss, you can set the expectation about work hours in an initial meeting. Then, if someone comes in late, it's easy for you to refer back to your conversation and say in a nonthreatening manner that they are not living up to the expectations you discussed. It's a way to take the emotion out of issues and deal with them professionally.

On the flip side, expectations meetings give your employees a way to address issues with you that may otherwise be uncomfortable for them. For example, if you told your employees that they should expect clear communication from you and they feel they aren't getting it, they can come to you and say, "Remember in our expectations meeting when we talked about communication? I'm finding some things unclear."

Note 1: Here are some questions you can address in your meeting. Keep in mind, these questions are asking for your employee's opinions, but they can serve as a starting point for you to talk about your expectations.

1. What do you want to get out of this job or assignment?
   This allows you to start a clear conversation about both your and your employee's goals.

2. What are some of the things you value in a working relationship?
   This allows you to understand how to best work with each other.

3. What kind of feedback do you find most helpful—written, verbal, immediately after a project or weekly?

Note 2: Be sure to write down everything that gets discussed in these meetings. Both you and your employee should walk away with a copy.

Watch out! Your employee may ask for some things that you cannot deliver. If it's something you wish you could do, or feel like you should do (even if you know you won't), you may be tempted to say that you will. That's a mistake. Don't promise something you won't do.

TIP #62
Keep employee files with detailed records

A little bit of paperwork and organization will save a ton of time and headaches in the unfortunate event you need to let someone go.

Neal Haber, an attorney with over thirty years of practice specializing in employment issues for Moss & Boris in New York City, says you should have an employee handbook or manual and get each employee to sign a receipt saying they've read it. That receipt needs to be kept in the employee's file.

In that same file, keep copies of documents concerning the employee, including their reviews. In addition, if you are having issues with an employee, keep precise notes (including dates and times and any relevant documents) explaining where the employee is falling short of his duties.

If you get to the point where you need to part ways with an employee, these documents will be critical to defend any questions about the termination decision. This becomes important when it comes to unemployment claims or if the employee decides to take legal action.

Important: It's also a good idea to keep detailed records of the good things your employee has done. This will help you give concrete examples of how they've added to the team during their yearly review.

Also important: Speaking of documents, Nina Kaufman from Ask the Business Lawyer says never pay a consultant without first getting them to fill out a W-9 form. You do not want to have to scramble to get people to fill out those documents at the end of the year when you have to turn them in!

TIP #63
Don't keep track of employee time off

If your company has a strong culture of company loyalty, instead of tracking sick and vacation days, just let your employees take time as they need it.

Barbara Weltman, founder of Big Ideas for Small Business in Millwood, New Jersey, says there are three benefits to running your company this way. First, employees appreciate it, which generally makes them more loyal to the company. Second, allotting a certain number of sick days actually encourages people to take them even if they are not sick. Finally, if someone who is really sick knows that she can take time off with pay, she'll stay home rather than come to work and infect everyone in the workplace!

Barbara finds that people rarely take advantage of this type of arrangement. In a well-run small business, everyone understands the importance of each person on the staff and how taking a day off puts a burden on someone else. In addition, she finds that such employees are much more willing to check in during their vacation if need be. Knowing that the company cares about you makes you care more about the company!

TIP #64
Cash in the credit card points

Problem: No money for employee bonuses

Solution: Don't forget your credit card points! Credit card points are an often forgotten and unused asset in a company. So when it comes to the end of the year, utilize them. Ellie Whalen, owner of New Jersey–based Sprayology, was extremely tight on cash a few years back. But she was rich in points. When it came time for employee bonuses, she traded in the points for gift cards. This move didn't touch her cash flow and she was still able to let her employees know she valued them.

CHAPTER FIVE

MANAGING PEOPLE

How to get the best from your employees

TIP #65 Insist on employee ownership of projects   96

TIP #66 Inject some fun into the office atmosphere   97

TIP #67 Give feedback (good and bad)
as it happens   98

TIP #68 Hold office hours for your employees   99

TIP #69 Set expectations high from the start   101

TIP #70 Share your company's accomplishments
at the end of every year   102

TIP #71 Fix performance issues by rewarding
the whole team   103

TIP #72 Create a help guide for your employees   105

TIP #73 Keep your staff focused on the right
priorities   106

TIP #74 Defer to your new managers   108

TIP #75 Decrease job-related injuries   110

TIP #76 Motivate your staff to pitch in with
one-off, annoying tasks   111

TIP #77 Perk up your office through some
inexpensive design   112

TIP #78 Keep your staff energized throughout
the day   114

TIP #65
Insist on employee ownership of projects

Never let an idea leave the room without a champion. My brother, Ken Ramberg, who has founded two successful companies, says that assigning ownership of a project or idea is the only way to ensure that something gets done (or at least fully evaluated—even if the result is to not move forward).

Someone needs to feel, and quite frankly be, responsible for pushing an idea forward. If a great idea does not get assigned an owner, chances are everyone will get so busy doing their own work that nothing will get done.

TIP #66
Inject some fun into the office atmosphere

Taking a little time off from your day-to-day work to have a little fun in the office goes a long way toward making your company a place where people are happy and eager to come to work. Here are a couple of "fun" suggestions:

Rodney Meeks, owner of Credit Consulting Services in Salinas, California, knows the stress his employees face making debt-collection calls all day long. To inject a bit of a distraction into this anxious atmosphere, one of his managers, Sharon Coles, asked everyone to bring in two photos—one of themselves as a child and one of their home. Rodney numbered the pictures and posted them on a bulletin board in the kitchen break area and then asked everyone to guess who belonged to each picture. The person with the most correct answers won fifty dollars. It gave everyone a nice pick-me-up, reducing the stress levels and reenergizing the staff.

At GoodSearch, we had everyone write down one thing about themselves that nobody would know. Someone then read them at our staff meeting and we all had to guess who it was. I must admit, the day we had this scheduled was an incredibly busy day for me. The idea of making our staff meeting run ten minutes longer seemed like a waste of time. But as it turned out, the exercise was so much fun that those extra ten minutes did more to lift my spirits and make me more productive than ten minutes more of work.

TIP #67
Give feedback (good and bad) as it happens

Don't wait for an employee review to let your employees know when they've done something great or not so great.

A thank-you from the boss is one of the most motivating pieces of feedback an employee can receive. A very detailed thank-you is even more valuable. Lolly Daskal, head of Lead from Within, in New York, explains that letting people know that they matter is incredibly simple but very meaningful. For example, instead of just saying "good job," Lolly might say, "Wow, your creativity helped us think outside the box. Thanks for not only your innovative thinking but for showing true leadership in expressing your ideas and pushing them through." That highlights the skills they used to achieve that job, which will encourage them to repeat the behavior in the future.

Even more motivating than a verbal thank-you is a handwritten note from you. Taking a couple of minutes to write something down shows your employee that you truly appreciate what they're doing.

On the flip side, when you feel an employee needs some help, have a timely conversation with them then too. Kenneth Trinder, CEO of EOS Surfaces, warns that you should never give criticism when you're feeling emotional or very disappointed. Always wait until you've been able to reflect on what you actually want to accomplish through giving the feedback.

TIP #68
Hold office hours for your employees

Problem: Your business has a large staff with several departments and you're so busy that you're losing touch with both your employees and what is happening in the day-to-day of your company.

Solution: Hold office hours once a week.

Remember office hours in college? It was the one time you could speak to your professor quietly and directly without a crush of other students waiting in line after class. Some business owners make a point of setting aside some time when anyone in the company can schedule a short meeting to talk about anything that concerns them. It's also a great way to get information about what's going on that you might not otherwise hear.

Case study 1: Susan Lyne, now chairperson of the Gilt Groupe in New York City, used this policy when she was CEO. She said she would leave open a two-hour block of time each week and encouraged her employees to book a half hour with her. Anyone in the company, from the receptionist to the VP of merchandising, could approach her. Susan says she benefited from these meetings in two ways. First, it gave her some insight into parts of her business that she wasn't able to spend a lot of time on. Second, it gave her a sense and feel for the mood at the company, which influenced how she and her top team managed the staff.

Case study 2: My mom, Connie Ramberg, did this same thing at her company, JobTrak, though she encouraged people to book as little as five minutes of time if that's all they

100 IT'S YOUR BUSINESS

wanted. Allowing such a short option gave employees who might have been intimidated by the idea of an entire half hour with the boss to feel like they could still get the chance to have some quality one-on-one time.

How I use this: At GoodSearch, our CEO, Scott Garell, puts aside one hour every week to simply walk around the office and talk to people. This is his way of checking in with everyone and seeing what they're working on and how they're feeling about the job. It's a really easy way to make our staff know that he's accessible and cares about what they're doing!

TIP #69
Set expectations high from the start

From day one, you must make it clear that you expect employees to do their very best work for you.

I learned to do this early on from a woman I worked with at Cooking.com during my first job after business school. Whenever anyone new who worked under her would hand in their first project, she would ask them, "Do you think this is absolutely complete and your best work?" She then would give the employee a chance to go back and fix their work (if it needed fixing).

The key to making this effective is that she would not look at the work before asking the question. That way it never came off as criticism. It was simply a question—and a strong signal that she did not want to take the time to review anything that was halfway done. And if someone said they wanted a couple more hours to look things over, she was happy to give it to them. Letting her direct reports know right from the start that she wanted top-notch work ensured that people were challenged to do their best. Everyone loved working for her because she set the bar high and supported people in reaching it.

Watch out! There is a very fine line between encouraging good work and being condescending. And it's all in the delivery. A condescending attitude from you will surely make your employees resent you.

TIP #70
*Share your company's accomplishments at
the end of every year*

Keep a list of all of your company's accomplishments each year and read the list at your holiday party. By the time December rolls around, most people forget what they did in January or February. This is a great way to wrap up the year and get everyone psyched to accomplish even more the next year.

How I use this: We have done this at GoodSearch since our first year, and now everyone looks forward to it. We work at a very fast pace and at times we are all so engrossed in our particular projects that we do not have the chance to step back, reflect, and see the big picture. Listing accomplishments is a really wonderful way to show how our company is growing, which in turn helps motivate everyone to keep on that track. It's also a wonderful team-building exercise! I keep an ongoing list and then read it out at our holiday party. It includes everything from how much money we raised for nonprofits that year to the key hires we made and big contracts we signed. I also put in fun, personal stuff as well, such as when my baby was born. This list also serves as a really fabulous company history that's fun and useful to look back on.

Watch out! If your company is going through a hard time, your accomplishments in a particular year may look paltry compared to those of a previous year. So make sure you frame everything in a positive light. For example, "In the worst recession since the Great Depression, we were still able to hang on to 60 percent of our clients."

Extra: This is a great list to share with investors or key partners of your company.

TIP #71
Fix performance issues by rewarding the whole team

Problem: Your staff is dropping the ball. Deadlines are being missed, orders are getting lost, or inventory is being mislabeled—it could be almost anything. The question is, how do you get your staff to stop bad habits and get back on track?

Solution: Motivate the department that is having problems to work together to solve the issue. How? Start by creating a chart where you can record how many incidents occur each day. Then offer a real reward to the entire unit if they can go for a certain period of time (days, weeks, or months) without a single incident. Be sure to make the reward worthwhile, such as a gift card for a popular store.

Case study: Zingerman's Delicatessen in Ann Arbor, Michigan, has a special catering division. When they started that division, the staff was having trouble scheduling all the different events they had been hired to cater. The owners were concerned because the weekly department reports indicated that they were actually missing or reporting late to events at least once a week, and sometimes even more often than that. So they offered each staff member in the department fifty dollars in cash if they could go fifty days with no late orders.

It didn't solve things right away, but it got the staff working as a team to figure out why they were dropping the ball. Eventually they smoothed out the kinks and managed to go fifty days without a late delivery. The owners then renewed the challenge and offered a bigger reward if the team could go for an entire year without incident. According to co-owner

Ari Weinzweig, the record is over four hundred days without a missed or late delivery. The key is that many of the systems and the culture of the department itself have changed drastically over the years, and that change was triggered in good part by the first challenge.

Scan to see a video

TIP #72
Create a help guide for your employees

Problem: As the owner of a business, especially in the beginning, you are the keeper of so much knowledge that answering employees' questions about how to do things can take up an inordinate amount of your time.

Solution: Derek Sivers, founder of CD Baby (which he sold for $22 million) in Portland, Oregon, decided that each time one of his twenty employees would ask him a routine question, he'd use it as a teaching moment. He'd gather the staff together, go through the answer, and ask someone to write it down. He was, in essence, creating the CD Baby bible, which people could refer to first before asking him anything. It also became the perfect training manual for new employees.

Watch out! Keep in mind, this type of document is only helpful if it's kept up-to-date. The best way to maintain it is to keep it online where everyone can access it and edit it, almost like a Wikipedia entry.

Good idea: I have found that it's good for employees who have regular tasks to create a "how to do my job" sheet with detailed instructions on what they do every day. When one of my employees recently left on vacation, she passed that sheet along to me and it was very easy to distribute her day-to-day work to the rest of the staff.

Scan to see a video

TIP #73
Keep your staff focused on the right priorities

Problem: You don't want to micromanage your staff, but you want to make sure everyone is focused on the right opportunities.

Solution: Tracy Randall, the CEO of Los Angeles–based Cooking.com (and my old boss), has a "daily check-in" with her management team where they each announce the top thing they are going to accomplish that day. Then, once a week, she has a quick meeting with each manager where they report on the top three things they're going to accomplish that week and that month. The managers go through this same routine with the members of their team.

This whole process takes just minutes but gives you the wherewithal to know what's going on in the office and to redirect anyone who is spending too much time on something that is not important to the business.

Sidebar: Danielle Snyder, cofounder of the New York company DANNIJO, says that since she's often out of the office, she keeps track of what everyone is doing by asking all of her employees to create "Friday Reports." These are quick e-mails sent at the end of the week updating Danielle on what was accomplished that week as well as on any concerns or ideas for improvements the employee has. These are not meant to be full-length reports, just quick bullet points to keep everyone in the know.

How I use this: When my brother and I hired Scott Garell as CEO of GoodSearch (after running it ourselves for five years), Scott implemented a "check-in" routine the very first month. I realized pretty quickly how much time I had been wasting trying to keep up with everyone's individual progress on my own. Once Scott had us start quickly listing our priorities, I saw how much time he saved himself.

TIP #74
Defer to your new managers

As your company grows and you hire new people to manage your current employees, your staff may find it hard to break their habit of coming directly to you for the final say.

Julie Chaiken, founder of Chaiken Clothing, ran her company for more than a decade when she decided to bring in David Lazar as CEO. She says the best way to support new management is to step out of the chain of command and let the new boss publicly have the final say. If you have a difference of opinion, express it only behind closed doors.

My experience: This happened to me early on in my career. I was one of the very first employees at a start-up called Cooking .com. After about a year or so of reporting directly to the CEO and COO, they brought in a vice president above me. But they also did something else that was smart. Soon after the VP came on board, I went into the COO's office to ask her a question and she told me that she didn't know the answer and that I should ask the VP. In retrospect, I realize that she absolutely knew the answer and could have resolved the issue with me right there. But she was training me to start reporting to my new boss. Seeing the COO defer to the new VP showed me, without me realizing it, that I should be doing the same.

How I use this: My brother (and co-founder) and I had a somewhat similar situation at GoodSearch, though on a larger scale, when we hired Scott Garell as our CEO after running GoodSearch ourselves for five years. Our employees were used to coming directly to us for everything. So early on, we had to let everyone know that Scott was now running the show—if we didn't, we'd be undermining his ability to lead the company. From his first day, Scott became the one in charge at staff meetings, and if we have any differences with him, we, like Julie, discuss it in private.

Scan to see a video

TIP #75
Decrease job-related injuries

Problem: Job-related injuries are scary! They are also expensive, harmful to morale, and can cause costly delays. So how do you get employees to stay conscious of personal safety during their daily shifts?

Solution: Reward people for staying safe.

Case study: Rachel and Andy Berliner, owners of Amy's Kitchen organic food company in Petaluma, California, run an ongoing company-wide contest encouraging job safety. At the end of each accident-free day, Rachel and Andy make a contribution to a special "safety fund." Once a month, they hold a contest for the best suggestion on how to improve workplace safety. The person who comes up with the best idea gets to spin a giant wheel of fortune and win a cash prize ranging from $100 to $500.

They say that this contest inspired employees to flag hazardous situations such as slippery floors and poor lighting before they could potentially cause an accident. These unsafe conditions might have gone unnoticed by management until it was too late, but the contest has kept the staff vigilant.

Added value: This is just one part of the Berliners' highly comprehensive safety program, which includes everything from redundant procedures for handling dangerous material to regular breaks for isometric exercises in order to prevent repetitive stress injuries. They say that since they've made safety a company priority, they have cut back significantly on injuries and their workers' compensation payments.

Scan to see a video

TIP #76
Motivate your staff to pitch in with one-off, annoying tasks

Problem: You've got a big, unexpected, timely, and tedious project (such as updating your database) that requires a lot of your staff's time.

Solution: If you don't want to outsource this work, turn it into a competition with a juicy reward for your employees.

How I use this: Last year, we sent out an e-mail to our mailing list asking them to update their addresses before we sent out their donation checks (at GoodSearch, we send out checks to our participating nonprofits and schools). We received an overwhelming response from organizations replying to make a change to their contact information—all of which had to be confirmed and manually updated (yes, in retrospect there was surely a better way to do this!).

We had one week to go through all of these e-mails and we needed everyone on our team to plow through them. So we took a day, split our staff into teams, and turned it into a contest to see which team could get through the most e-mails. The winning team won a day at the spa. This turned a totally tedious task into something that became a fun, team-building exercise.

TIP #77
Perk up your office through some inexpensive design

No one likes working in a dreary-looking office. If the atmosphere is sufficiently drab, it can demoralize your staff. Conversely, a nicely designed office can energize everyone who works there. Designer Tom Vecchione, a principal at the design firm Gensler, has a couple of inexpensive tricks to perk up the atmosphere in any office:

- Buy some inexpensive bar stools and a tall table to create a work bar. This allows your employees to move around the office and to work standing up with their laptop or have a group meeting standing up. If you place this near a window, it also gives employees who don't have a window view the chance to see some outside scenery.

- Add a little color to your office. While there is a lot of theory about how colors affect people, Tom says to go with the color palette of your logo in order to create a cohesive brand experience. You don't have to paint every single wall—consider just painting one wall, or, if you have columns, paint the columns.

- Create your own art. Tom suggests taking clever photos of your employees, blowing them up large, and then hanging them from wires with binder clips. Or, frame your logo in different sizes to create an interesting display.

How I use this: The art in the GoodSearch office all comes from GoodSearch.com. On our homepage, we have a series of beautiful photographs that represent the causes we support. We've blown up those photographs with our logo and use them to decorate the walls. It reminds everyone of our mission the minute we walk through the door. Not to mention, we already paid for the photographs to use for the site, so we're getting double duty out of them!

Extra tip: When my mom first started her company, JobTrak, she got some canvas and painted a bunch of pictures that were basically Mondrian-like squares of colors. Keep in mind my mother was by no means a professional artist. But once she framed her paintings, they did a lot to liven up the office!

TIP #78
Keep your staff energized throughout the day

By the end of the day, people are often a little less on their game. So how do you keep them energized all afternoon? Here are a couple of ideas.

Andrew Shapiro, founder of New York–based Green-Order, schedules regular five-minute team stretching breaks out on the company's terrace. This has become a much-beloved ritual that not only helps people make it through the rest of the day, but also helps strengthen the culture of his company.

James Curleigh, the CEO of KEEN, takes this one step farther, bringing back the idea of recess. Each member of his staff is encouraged to take a ten-minute recess...whether that's stretching on a yoga mat, playing Frisbee, using a hula hoop, or hopping on a bike (he gives his employees a list of local places where they can do these activities). Everyone then tracks their activities, and their "recess" accomplishments are celebrated by management.

At GoodSearch, we keep healthy food in the office. Since we work pretty long hours, everyone always needs a snack during the day. As it turns out, we all pretty much eat whatever happens to be there. If that's candy, we'll eat that. If it's carrots, we'll eat that. As a result, we now make sure we have more carrots around than cookies. Unhealthy food full of sugar often causes people to become dull and sluggish toward the end of the day, so make sure there are always healthy alternatives around.

Rodney Meeks, owner of Credit Consulting Services, took this idea one step farther. He challenged anyone on his staff who wanted to participate to lose 10 percent of their body weight. The ones who signed up were assigned health-buddies to help keep themselves on the program. He says this resulted in a more alert staff and more satisfied individuals.

Tip: Since we're on the subject of food, here's one tidbit someone told me—always make it a habit to clean out the office refrigerator on Fridays. Wait any longer than that, and it just gets filled with spoiled food.

CHAPTER SIX

CLOSING THE SALE

Selling your goods or services

TIP #79   Cater to your customers' emotional needs   118

TIP #80   Send a package that begs to be opened   119

TIP #81   Change your tone of voice to make a sale   120

TIP #82   Never give a price over the phone   121

TIP #83   Don't agree to lower your price
without changing the terms   122

TIP #84   Don't decrease price; increase value   123

TIP #85   Find out your customer's budget   124

TIP #86   Get past the corporate gatekeeper   125

TIP #87   Close the sale with open-ended questions   126

TIP #88   Connect with your sales prospects by
"mirroring"   128

TIP #89   Find good sales reps   129

TIP #90   Call your leads within fifteen minutes   130

TIP #91   Set up multiple price points   132

TIP #92   Be strategic about where you place
products in your store   134

TIP #93   Keep store shelves stocked even when
you can't afford it   135

TIP #94	Get to the right buyers at big retailers	136
TIP #95	Point out product flaws to make your sale	137
TIP #96	Trade Show 101	138
TIP #97	How to stand out at a trade show without a booth	140
TIP #98	Market your service as "solving a problem"	141
TIP #99	Upsell your customers	143
TIP #100	Use an odd number—it's more memorable	145

TIP #79
Cater to your customers' emotional needs

Case study: This is the insight that helped Paul Orfalea turn a tiny copy shop in Southern California called Kinko's into an international brand that he sold to FedEx for a major undisclosed figure.

Paul says that almost from the beginning, he realized that while he was selling photocopies for a nickel apiece, he was really in the business of assuaging people's anxieties. Many of his customers were coming in at the last minute with application forms, college term papers, legal documents, manuscripts, and résumés. They were facing deadlines, needed a job to be done, and they needed it done yesterday!

Once Paul understood the emotional needs of his customers, he got his employees to focus their attention on being patient and providing guidance as well as photocopies. He also provided free access to office supplies such as staplers, Scotch Tape, and even free coffee so people would not be frustrated that they didn't have the correct supplies on hand to finish their task. This relatively simple observation, he says, was the key to growing the business.

TIP #80
Send a package that begs to be opened

Problem: You're trying to get someone who receives mountains of product pitches or proposals to pay attention to yours.

Solution: Send a package that begs to be opened.

Case study: Kristy Engels of New York–based Hair Rules went to a conference specifically to meet the buyer of a store where she wanted to sell her product. Her plan was to give her product pitch in person and then follow up with samples in the mail. When Kristy gave her pitch and asked for the address, the buyer responded with a curt shrug and said, "Good luck getting my attention" because she had several closets filled with unopened sample boxes.

Undaunted, Kristy went to Tiffany and bought a hundred-dollar crystal bowl to fill with her products—a small price to pay for snagging a new and important client. But the trick wasn't actually the crystal bowl itself. The key to her plan was having the box sent directly from Tiffany. So instead of receiving another dull package in the mail, the buyer received a pretty blue box addressed to her. As you can imagine, that one got opened!

In fact, the buyer took the box home and opened it with her family, since she thought it was a personal item sent to her office by mistake. Kristy's Hair Rules products got the buyer's full attention, and the woman was so impressed that she's been a client ever since.

TIP #81
Change your tone of voice to make a sale

Tone of voice definitely matters, whether you're making a presentation or making a sale.

Phoenix real estate agent Brett Barry says he learned an important lesson while taking voice lessons during high school. He says a change in your voice inflection at a key moment can be your silver bullet!

When he's taking a couple around to look at houses, he sometimes senses that they are very close to making a decision. At that point, he says he'll change his voice for one key comment. Speaking in a barely audible whisper, which forces them to pay close attention, he'll say something like, "I really love this house," or "Ahh, this house is wonderful."

When he can see the couple is going through their mental checklist, and one of them might say, "I really love the kitchen," and the other might say, "The garage is a perfect size," and they're obviously considering the home, that's when he'll make his whispered comment, often tipping the scale to make the sale.

This works, he insists, because it causes two things to happen. The hushed tone of voice focuses their attention on the moment, and the whispered message makes them confirm and recognize what they are both thinking unconsciously.

Scan to see a video

TIP #82
Never give a price over the phone

Never give specific prices for your service over the phone.

Customers constantly price-shop. Don't turn them off with prices that are too high or too low. If you are cornered by someone who demands a price, state a wide range. It's important for customers to really understand what you do before they evaluate your service. So before you give them a number, explain to them what they are getting for their money.

Case study: Eli Natan, CEO of the Los Angeles–based Promoting Group, had a potential client who called inquiring about marketing services, and the first question he asked was, "How much do you charge?" The person who answered the phone replied, "Our services range from one thousand to fifteen thousand dollars monthly, on retainer, depending on the service and how much time we spend on the account."

That answer made the prospective client interested and he scheduled a meeting to see what the different price ranges would offer. If they had quoted him the $15,000-a-month service cost, he probably would have hung up the phone. By providing a price range, it helped them to find his monthly marketing budget at $5,000 a month and provide a custom solution that worked for his specific business needs.

TIP #83
Don't agree to lower your price without changing the terms

Problem: A customer asks for a lower price. You don't want to lose the sale, but you don't want to lower your price. What do you do?

Solution: Any time the customer says "I need a lower price," Thomas Nagle, a partner at Boston-based The Monitor Group, says you should put the ball back in their court and say something like, "Tell me what price you need it to be."

They will then tell you what budget you're working with. You can then take a positive approach by saying, "OK, here are three things you can do to get that price: (1) you can take a different service package, (2) you can guarantee more volume, or (3) you can pay for it in cash (or whatever kind of concession you think will make the price reduction worthwhile).

Extra benefit: By sticking to a negotiation that follows along these lines with that customer, he or she will soon realize that every time he asks for a price reduction, he will be asked to give something back in exchange. Without a policy like this in place, many people find themselves on the slippery slope of new price-reduction requests each time the customer returns to make his next purchase.

TIP #84
Don't decrease price; increase value

One of the first reactions to a slump in sales is to discount prices. This is a very dangerous move. Unless you were charging too much in the first place, you may be lowering your prices to the point of affecting your profitability. After doing that, it will be very difficult to move your prices back to where you actually need them to be.

Instead of decreasing your prices, add to the value of your products.

One of the best ways to enhance sales is to increase the perception of the value of your products. Julia Kushnir of Tax Solutions in Nyack, New York, says you should make sure your product stands out and, in addition, be sure to add some sort of bonus value that is hard to compare with what competitors offer. These sorts of "value-added" elements should be of little additional cost to you but should change the way the consumer perceives your product.

Case study: Michael Bagley, owner of Fav's Treatery in Florida, New York, bundles a cup of coffee with one of his four-dollar Bruffins, and charges five dollars for both. Usually the coffee goes for more than a dollar. So he's discounted the coffee but maintained the price of the Bruffin, a costlier product to produce.

TIP #85
Find out your customer's budget

In most cases, knowing a prospect's budget is critical to making a sale.

Once you have a budget range, you can figure out what products to present and whether that prospect is even worth your time. But directly asking "What is your budget" will probably get you a wishy-washy answer such as "I'm not sure," or "I don't really have one." Robert Levin, founder of the *New York Enterprise Report*, gave us the following alternative questions you can use to get at that key information:

- "Assuming that our product/service is a good fit for you, could you give us a range of what kind of investment you could afford?"

- "Some of our clients in your space spend between $5,000 and $10,000 and some between $10,000 and $15,000. Which range does your company fit in?"

- "Our product runs from between $5,000 and $15,000, depending on several factors. If we together determine that we can help you, is something within that range affordable?"

TIP #86
Get past the corporate gatekeeper

Problem: You need to reach a decision maker at a large firm.

Solution: Call or e-mail them when their assistants are not working.

When he was starting out, Jean-Luc Neptune, of New York–based ExpertConsensus, found he couldn't get past gatekeepers such as assistants when he was trying to reach key decision makers. Often, senior executives have assistants who serve as a buffer, screening e-mails and phone calls.

The best way to reach those senior executives is to contact them when the assistants are not at their desks. Phone calls before eight a.m. and after six p.m. are much more likely to be answered directly by your target, and e-mails sent on the weekend and late at night are much more likely to be seen and answered directly as well.

TIP #87
Close the sale with open-ended questions

The standard advice to salespeople is to know all the answers to all the questions about your product. Of course, that's great advice, but according to Terry Miller of Galpin Motors, who is one of the highest-earning car salesmen in Los Angeles, the real secret to closing a sale isn't knowing the answers, it's asking the right questions.

Terry says if you ask open-ended questions, you can accomplish two vital tasks that will help you make the sale. First, you establish a friendly relationship with your prospect by showing that you're interested in them as a person, and that builds trust. "How's your family?" "Do you live around here?" "What do you plan to do with your new car?"

Second, and even more important, he says, asking these questions allows you to learn vital information about your client that you can use later to close the sale. In one example, Terry says his customer casually mentioned having a large pet dog at home and right away, he used this information to steer his customer to the SUV section with cars large enough to accommodate the pet. They quickly closed the deal.

How I use this: I recently met with the senior managers of a company to propose a partnership with GoodSearch. Instead of walking in and pitching them my proposal, I spent the first half hour of the conversation asking them about their strategic goals. As a result of the information I learned, I was able to tailor my pitch to them.

Early on in my career, I was often so wed to the scripted proposals that I had prepared based on what I *thought* someone would be interested in accomplishing that I would forget to take the time to actually listen to what they were *truly* interested in accomplishing.

Scan to see a video

TIP #88
Connect with your sales prospects by "mirroring"

When you and your customer are on the same wavelength, it seems so easy to close the sale. The problem is that you're not always on the same wavelength with everyone you meet. Menina Givens, a top Mary Kay independent sales force member, taught us how she uses "mirroring" to connect with her prospects.

She subtly mirrors the body language and the mood of the person to whom she's speaking. If someone is excited, she gets excited. If they speak softly, she does the same. If they seem astonished, she finds something to be astonished about too. If they lean in toward her, she leans in too.

Research findings: This sales tip comes out of the groundbreaking social science research of Tanya Chartrand, of Duke University, and John Bargh, now at Yale University. They examined the impact of people's natural tendencies to imitate one another's speech and body movement. They called their findings the "Chameleon Effect," and sales experts have found this research to be highly useful.

Watch out! When it comes to mirroring another person's tone of voice or body movements, be careful not to overdo it. Be subtle. If they cross their legs, pause a few moments before crossing yours; if they use certain words, use some of those same words in your comments, but don't parrot everything they say.

Scan to see a video

TIP #89
Find good sales reps

When looking for a sales rep, you want to find someone who already has relationships with your potential customer base. After all, if you can find someone with the right connections, it will absolutely speed up your time to market. So how do you find those people—especially if you're new to the industry?

A. K. L'Heureux, the founder of Hyde, a New York–based yoga-wear company, says to look for people who already represent products that are complementary to yours. For example, since she was new to selling yoga clothing, A.K. looked for sales reps who sold yoga equipment, such as mats, and asked them to rep her products as well.

It's really not that hard to find these reps. Simply go to a retailer you'd like to work with and ask them for the name of the person who sells them those complementary products. This may take a little legwork, as many of these manufacturers may not use outside reps, but with enough asking, you'll find some leads.

Tip: Laura Galbraith, an experienced sales rep, often gets swamped by calls from producers like A.K. who want her to take on new products. Laura says she doesn't automatically say yes. She needs to be convinced that (1) the products will meet the standards her clients expect, and (2) the company can reliably fill the orders. The last thing a sales rep wants is to promise a client something only to find that the company she's representing can't deliver!

TIP #90
Call your leads within fifteen minutes

Phone all sales leads from your website or voice mail within fifteen minutes, if possible.

Leanne Hoagland-Smith, who has her own consulting company in Valparaiso, Indiana, says that she has converted over 75 percent of her sales leads by responding within that key fifteen-minute time frame. While this is certainly a challenge for salespeople who are incredibly busy, it clearly pays off in dividends.

Research supports Hoagland-Smith's idea. James Oldroyd, of SKK Graduate School of Business, in collaboration with MIT Sloan, studied the topic of lead-response management and found that Wednesdays and Thursdays are the best days to make contact with someone and that between four and six p.m. is the best time. But calling back as quickly as possible is far more important than sticking to any of these days or times. According to that study, your odds of reaching a lead drops one hundred times if you wait thirty minutes versus five minutes.

Why is this?

Well, when someone provides an online lead, chances are they're still in that same spot five minutes later. If they just called, they're probably still near their phone and not in a meeting. Secondly, you're getting in touch with them right when they need something, since they just made contact. If you wait too long, they may not be interested anymore. And thirdly, there is something the researchers called the "Wow Effect." In essence, when you get back to someone quickly, they often have the reaction "Wow—

that was fast! You are impressive," which makes your company seem like the kind of business they want to work with.

You can see the whole study here: http://www.leadresponse management.org/lrm_study

TIP #91
Set up multiple price points

Problem: What should you charge for your goods or services? You don't want to price yourself out of the market, but you don't want to charge too little.

Background: According to Thomas Nagle, the author of *The Strategy and Tactics of Pricing*, there have been a number of very helpful studies done on this question. These studies suggest that the smart way to go is to have several price points and let your customers decide for themselves what they want to spend.

Think about how automobile manufacturers have compacts, midsize, and full-size luxury models in addition to SUVs and sports cars. They offer something different for every taste and pocketbook. That way, it doesn't matter if your customer is a "show-off" who only wants the top of the line, or a "tightwad" who wants to pay as little as possible. You've got something to fit their budget within your single shop.

Nagle says when customers are buying products that they don't buy on a regular basis (such as cars, jewelry, computers, etc.) they rely heavily on the price as an indicator of the level of quality of the product.

Solution: More often than not, customers make their decision about what price they're willing to pay based less on the features and benefits of the products and more on their own established habits of buying. If they are used to buying the "top of the line," that's what they'll do when they buy from you. Similarly, if someone is on a tight budget, they will seek out the lower-priced items because that's what they feel they can afford. The vast majority of customers won't fall into either of those categories; they will tend to go for the medium price, based on their habits of looking for adequate quality for best price.

That being said, you should offer a price range of low, medium, and high. If you want to encourage people to go for the next higher level, you might consider adding a new price tier that could be called "super high." Doing this won't necessarily generate a lot of sales in that super-high category, but it will likely have the ripple effect of pulling some of the medium-range customers into the formerly high range, and some of the low-range customers into the formerly medium range.

In fact, Nagle says, sometimes manufacturers will go so far as to build a version of their product with a lot of extra bells and whistles just for this purpose. They do this to encourage customers to raise their tolerance for the cost of the next highest product. The reverse of this thinking comes into play with wine lists at restaurants. People generally don't want to buy the cheapest wine on the list, and as such, will tend to buy the next cheapest. So the price of the cheapest makes the price of the next cheapest more acceptable.

Whatever you do, Nagle warns, remember that there are always more people trying to get adequate quality at a low price than the best quality at any price. So if you have only two price levels, the lower price level will sell in greater volume than the higher. That's why you want to have at least three price levels.

If you want to dive a bit deeper into the theory behind all this, I urge you to pick up a copy of Nagle's book. The psychology of pricing is fascinating.

TIP #92
Be strategic about where you place products in your store

As your customers browse through the aisles of your store, you have only a few seconds at best to capture their eyes and to motivate them to pick up an item to put in their basket. Bob Sickles, of his namesake grocery store in Little Silver, New Jersey, offers some very basic to-dos when setting out the layout of your store and products:

• Put your best sellers right at eye level. This way even your most distracted customers won't miss them.

• Different eye levels catch different customers. Moms have different eye levels than kids. Sickles places the lollipops and colorful toys in buckets near the floor, while the catsup and dish soap are placed higher up. Place top sellers in more than one location. For example, in addition to putting olive oil where customers expect to find it, in the summer he also puts some in the produce section near the tomatoes. He always keeps the doughnuts near the baked-goods section, but in the fall he puts them near the apple cider case as well.

• Put the most commonly purchased items toward the back of the store. Since so many people buy milk and eggs, putting them in the back helps draw customers through the aisles to get to them. This way, people are forced to pass by the rest of the products, often leading them to buy something else as well.

Scan to see a video

TIP #93
Keep store shelves stocked even when you can't afford it

Problem: You don't have enough money to stock your retail store's shelves.

Solution: Fake it!

Case study: Arthur Blank and Bernie Marcus are the masterminds behind The Home Depot. But these pioneers had almost no money for merchandise when they opened the doors to their first store in 1978.

Falling far short of their vision of having customers overwhelmed with a variety of products, the founders, along with merchandising genius Pat Farrah, came up with a solution for filling their empty floor-to-ceiling shelves: They simply faked it! Bernie and Arthur improvised at the last minute by asking their paint supplier for empty paint cans, and their other merchandise suppliers for extra boxes. Everything above arm's reach was empty, and everything below was real. But the appearance of a fully stocked superstore was intact, and the rest is history...

Scan to see a video

TIP #94
Get to the right buyers at big retailers

Reaching a buyer at a large company who specializes in your type of product is not impossible if you know a couple of tricks.

Karen Waksman, president of Product for Profit, says first you have to find the name and contact information of the right person. Unfortunately, for many big companies, it's not as easy as just calling and asking the company operator. They may connect you to a voice mail for a buyer, but not necessarily the right buyer.

Karen says a better way to find the right contact is to check out *The Chain Store Guide* and *The Salesman's Guide*, both of which compile this contact information. There's just one catch—those books are quite expensive. If you live in a major city, check out the reference section in your local library. Suddenly, you'll be able to get all the key information you need for free! One thing to note—make sure you're looking at an edition that is less than a year old, as buyers tend to move around a lot.

Karen also says never call a buyer on a Monday. That's the day they go over their numbers and generally have team meetings—as a new seller, you don't want to catch a buyer when they're distracted and potentially annoyed by your call.

TIP #95
Point out product flaws to make your sale

When you're talking with a potential customer, it might seem natural to focus only on the positives and to brush over the negatives.

But that's just plain wrong according to Brett Barry, a real estate agent with more than seventeen years of experience. He says he always makes sure to point out a few flaws or downsides to the properties he's showing, which helps him engender trust and close the deal faster.

Brett, who has sold more than eight hundred houses in his career, says that pointing out a flaw or two lets him show, right off the bat, that he's realistic and objective about the property he's trying to sell. And more than that, he says when you point out a few of the property's downsides, your client will more likely believe you when you point out the benefits.

TIP #96
Trade Show 101

So you've splurged this year and decided to attend your industry trade show. Make the most out of this big investment by following these tips from Dan Cohen of Clearbrook Farms in Sharonville, Ohio, and Bill Lynch, senior director of membership and exhibitions at the Fancy Food Show, in New York City:

• **Don't leave the booth!** You are there to meet people, so make sure you are in the booth when that all-important customer stops by. You usually get only one shot, and if you miss them, it may be another year (at the next year's trade show) before you get the chance to have another face-to-face meeting. Insiders tell us they actually choose their booth space at large venues such as the Javits Center in New York based on bathroom proximity! This means strategically planning a booth space that isn't a ten-minute walk to a bathroom. Don't leave to have lunch, either. Pack snacks and eat discreetly when there is a lull in the action. Dan Cohen tells us you don't want a list of "be-backs." "Be-backs" usually never get the opportunity to "be back," even when they intend to.

• **Never sit down!** Bill always tells exhibitors they've got three seconds to capture the attention of an attendee walking by. It sounds simple, but you should be smiling, looking people in the eye, and clearly happy to be there. Too often, you see people hiding at the back of the booth, yawning and checking their watches. This gives off negative cues and will quickly turn people away. If you are staffing the booth with your employees, make sure you select people who have the right personality, energy, and staying power to represent your company in a positive way.

- **Quickly follow up leads!** Dan says your work isn't done when the trade show is over. He says the biggest mistake people make after exhibiting at a trade show is not following up leads. That means quickly getting samples out and starting an e-mail correspondence.

How I use this: GoodSearch had a booth a few years in a row at the Association of Fundraising Professionals conference. While we were staffing the booth, my employees and I made a game out of getting people's attention—setting a goal of not letting one single person walk by without at least trying to get them to talk to us. Admittedly, this was exhausting. But it was also fun. It's amazing how many people will stop and talk if you just engage them with a hello.

Scan to see a video

TIP #97
How to stand out at a trade show without a booth

Problem: You want to attend your industry trade show without renting a booth space.

Solution: Throw a party instead!

Colin Schiller at Gotham Software in New York says one way to effectively use trade show dollars is to set up a private party or large group dinner and use the velvet-rope strategy like a hip nightclub. Work hard to get a few high-profile people to attend and then make it "invite only" so that others will want to come.

This will give you a great chance to spend focused time with the people you really want to contact. Also, it will build positive buzz for your business when everyone starts talking about your cool event. If the party is too expensive to do on your own, find a partner to co-sponsor it. This can help defray the cost and should lead to an even better attendee list when your contact lists are combined.

TIP #98
Market your service as "solving a problem"

When marketing our products and services, most of us tend to focus solely on the benefits. But small business owner and consultant Barry Moltz in Chicago says that people are much more apt to buy painkillers than vitamins—so let your customers know what kind of pain your business kills and they'll have a whole new way of thinking about your business.

Case study: Barry was a panelist on a recent *Your Business* broadcast where that day's "elevator pitcher" told us about her product—a light-up menu for dark restaurants. She went on to talk about the benefits of diners being able to see their choices. Barry's feedback to her was that she needed to reframe the pitch to talk about the "pain" the restaurant is feeling and how this menu solves it.

For example, the restaurant owner may be suffering from complaints from patrons that it's too dark to read the menu; complaints from waiters that they are wasting a lot of time talking about what's on the menu to people who can't see it; and complaints from waiters that they have to carry around flashlights, which get lost or run out of batteries.

Once you've highlighted a customer's problem, you can then talk about how your product solves it. Talking about a pain versus a benefit may be a subtle distinction, but Barry says this change in framing makes all the difference.

How I use this: I've had a lot of meetings with organizations to talk to them about incorporating GoodSearch into their corporate social-responsibility planning. Each company that I speak to has a different goal—in essence a different pain they're trying solve. Some want to make their employees happy; some want to focus on getting more customers; some simply feel like they'd like to do some good for the community. Before I go into any of these meetings, I try to best understand their "pain" and then tailor my pitch to it. And, if I'm not able to understand it ahead of time, I ask the potential partner to explain their goals in the beginning of my meeting so I can change my pitch on the fly.

TIP #99
Upsell your customers

A little dessert after dinner? Free shipping if you spend just ten dollars more? Buy one, get the second one half-off? All of this is *upselling*—getting the customer to splurge on a bit more than they planned. According to Steve Strauss, author of *The Small Business Bible*, there are five simple rules to upselling. And, if you do it right, it's a win-win for you and your customers.

• **Wait until the sale is over:** If you make the offer while the customer is still deciding on the primary purchase, it will feel pushy and could backfire. If you wait, it looks like you're merely offering great customer service.

• **Make it affordable:** A five-dollar add-on to a ninety-nine-dollar product may be no big deal but a five-dollar "extra" on a fifteen-dollar product is a whole other story. Upselling works best when the offer is a small addition to the larger purchase.

• **Be casual about it:** Upselling works in a friendly, no-pressure way. "Want some ice cream on that apple pie?" "A side of fries with that burger?" When it's not a hard sell, it works well.

• **Point out the benefits:** The customer already wants the item they're buying. For the add-on to work, it should make sense. If they're buying charcoal, the odds are good they'll also want lighter fluid. They belong together. If your suggestion is thoughtful, the customer will be glad you made the proposal.

- **Consider "bundling":** If you sell computer printers you can create a bundle that might include extra toner cartridges, fancy photo paper, special cleaning wipes, etc., all combined at a price below the individual costs of the separate items. You've increased your sale and the customer gets a deal on extra stuff for their primary purchase. It's another form of upselling.

TIP #100
Use an odd number—it's more memorable

If you want something to be noticed, use an odd number instead of an even number.

. This trick comes in handy when you're trying to capture a customer's attention. Odd numbers get noticed more than even ones, according to Rieva Lesonsky, founder of GrowBiz Media in Lakewood, California. She says if you're offering a package of your top-selling items, don't make it a top 10 (or 100) list—they've become all too common and expected. (Don't say nine or ninety-nine either; that just sounds like you've left something out.) So what number should you use? Rieva says numbers like "The Top 11" or "103 Best-Selling Items" make what you're selling more noticeable and memorable.

She goes on to say that if you're really daring (and not superstitious), try using the number thirteen. Most people shy away from thirteen, so if you're bold enough to use it, you'll definitely stand out from the crowd.

How I use this: Check out how many tips there are in this book. A random, odd number! (By the way, the irony is not lost on us that this ended up being tip 100!)

CHAPTER SEVEN

CULTIVATING CUSTOMERS

Getting and keeping your customers

TIP #101 Turn no into yes—part one   149

TIP #102 Turn no into yes—part two   150

TIP #103 When negotiating, keep something
in your back pocket   152

TIP #104 Get qualified customer leads   153

TIP #105 Never put down competitors   154

TIP #106 Improve your employees' phone skills   156

TIP #107 Don't underestimate the value of a
handwritten card   157

TIP #108 Go on a "listening tour" to learn
what your clients need   158

TIP #109 Never say no to a potential customer   159

TIP #110 Find common interests with
your customer   160

TIP #111 Anticipate a nonpaying customer   162

TIP #112 Set time boundaries with your clients   164

TIP #113 Keep the "extras" in check   165

TIP #114 Use your customers as advisors   166

TIP #115 Get your customers to help you
improve your new products   167

TIP #116   Use mistakes to engender loyalty   168

TIP #117   Segment your customers into
            three categories   170

TIP #118   Respond to negative customer
            feedback positively   172

TIP #119   End customer interactions on a
            positive note   174

TIP #120   Tap into social media data   175

TIP #121   Make your customer surveys count   176

TIP #122   Connect to customers with QR codes   178

TIP #123   Get your holiday gift noticed   180

TIP #124   Answer the phone   181

TIP #125   Don't give away professional
            advice for free   182

TIP #126   Let customers know you listened
            to them   183

TIP #127   Reduce your no-shows   185

TIP #128   Fire your customers   186

TIP #101
Turn no into yes—part one

If a potential client has ultimately decided he or she does not need or want your services, don't let this be the end of the relationship. Keep their need or project in mind and contact them after a week or so with a piece of advice or an article or something that relates to their project. You can start the e-mail by saying that you "just happened to come across this while working on something else and thought they would be interested." This should not be a solicitation for their business, but simply a friendly e-mail. This can set the groundwork for a future relationship or keep you at the top of their mind in case something goes wrong with their current service provider.

Case study: Ashlie Yair from New York–based A.Y. Dzyne used this technique and gained a client as a result. She does event design and had a potential client who was interested in hiring her to do a child's "princess" birthday party. Ashlie put together a proposal, but the client politely responded that she had decided to do the planning herself.

About a week later, Ashlie did a little research and sent the woman a link to a castle tent that she found online for twenty dollars. She included a note saying, "Hi, I hope all is going smoothly with your party planning. I came across this castle while working on another event and I thought it would be great for your party."

The next day, the woman sent Ashlie an e-mail thanking her for the link and asking if she was still available to plan the event. Just a few minutes of Ashlie's time secured her a new job!

TIP #102
Turn no into yes—part two

Problem: A customer or potential customer says no to your offer.

Solution: Don't think of that no as "never." Think of it as "not now." Needs change as circumstances change and you don't want to be shut out of a possible deal because you never circled back to a potential partner or sales prospect.

Jenny Fulton, co-owner of Miss Jenny's Pickles in Kernersville, North Carolina, says that you should give yourself a reminder to call your target at some point in the future. Put it in your calendar with detailed notes about why they rejected your offer the first time and develop some ideas about new approaches to use when you speak to them again.

How I use this: When we first launched GoodSearch, a large animal-rights group was one of the only nonprofits that did not want to work with us. For four years, I called my contact every three to six months, often knowing that she was still going to say that she was not ready to work with us. For all those years I was so busy that I often forgot about the organization, but then I'd get a reminder on my calendar that I had previously scheduled for myself.

Each time I had a conversation with her, I was able to better understand her objections so that I could address them in our next call (you should see my notes from these conversations—they're pages long!).

In addition, I was able to build up a really nice relationship with my contact there. You can only imagine how excited I was when I got the call that they were ready to sign up with

GoodSearch! In the end, I believe this long-term relationship is what helped them to change their mind as much as anything else.

I always refer to this experience when I hire new people. It would have been easy, after four years, to give up on them. But it didn't take much of my time, just a lot of persistence.

Scan to see a video

TIP #103
When negotiating, keep something in your back pocket

The best way to impress a new client is to over-deliver. One of the surest ways to over-deliver is to under promise in a negotiation. By under promise, we don't mean sell your skills or services short, we mean keep a little something in your back pocket that you can give your client for free once the deal is done.

Neil Vogel, who founded and ran the Webby Awards and Internet Week for nearly a decade in New York, says that whenever he's doing a deal with a new sponsor or advertiser, he always tries to hold back on telling them about a little something extra he can do. That could be more ads on his site, free tickets to events, or extra exposure. Once the deal is done and he's secured the client, he wows them with the extras.

Tip: Neil says not to let the client know about these "extras" right away. You can use them throughout the deal to keep the client surprised and happy!

TIP #104
Get qualified customer leads

What if you could have access to *all* of your competitor's customers?

When a competitor goes out of business, immediately call the phone company and ask to have their number redirected to yours. What better way to get qualified leads! Mike Michalowicz, the New Jersey–based founder of Obsidian Launch and author of *The Pumpkin Plan*, says that you'll have to train your staff to politely explain that the company they intended to reach has gone out of business and that you can provide them with excellent service.

This advice holds for URLs as well. A competitor who has closed up shop may be willing to sell their web address to you at a reasonable price. Or you could strike a deal to have their URL redirect to yours in return for paying for leads that come to your site via that channel.

TIP #105
Never put down competitors

It's bad form to put down a competitor. Quite frankly, people are put off by it. So how can you make it clear that you provide better service or products? Norm Brodsky, founder of New York–based CitiStorage (which he sold for $110 million in 2007), said this is how he does it:

> **Potential client:** "I am looking at working with you, or company A or company B."
> **Norm:** "I have not heard of company B, but I am very familiar with company A."

According to Norm, by simply saying you are not familiar with company B, this immediately discredits them with the potential client.

> **Norm:** "Company A is an excellent company with a good reputation."

According to Norm, complimenting your competitor makes you more believable and your opinions more credible.

> **Norm:** "Here is why I believe we could provide you the best service."

This is where you list all of your qualifications. Do not blatantly put down company A, but rather talk about how good you are.

Norm: "As you continue this process, if you learn of something that another company does that you believe we do not offer, please check back with me. Chances are it's a part of what we already do or what we can do for you as well."

This gives you the chance to rebut anything your competition says about why they are better than you.

TIP #106
Improve your employees' phone skills

A smile translates over phone lines. So it's important for your employees—especially your customer service and sales teams—to smile, stay upbeat, and remain helpful when on the phone. My mom, Connie Ramberg, the founder of JobTrak—a company that succeeded because of its excellent customer service—found a simple way to ensure that this happened.

How? She put a mirror on everyone's desk and told them to be sure to glance at it when they were on the phone to make sure they were smiling. Now, of course she did not truly believe that everyone would stare at themselves in the mirror each time they were on the phone, but it did serve as a physical reminder to be cheerful when dealing with customers.

Added tip: Get your own mirror too. As a small business owner, you are responsible for forging relationships—whether that's in a meeting, at a party, or perhaps while giving a speech for your industry. Business coach Lolly Daskal says that all too often our facial expression is communicating something different than our thoughts—and because people read your face as an emotional response, it's important that your face convey a message of engagement rather than something negative. This is easy to do. Simply stand in front of a mirror or videotape yourself pretending to talk to someone and check to see if your expressions are reflecting the emotions you want. It may sound basic, but trust me, it works. And it's important.

TIP #107
Don't underestimate the value of a handwritten card

A handwritten note in the age of voice mail, e-mail, and social media easily breaks through the noise, is a lot more personal, and is a simple way to show the person you care.

So make sure to write a simple handwritten thank-you card after meeting with a new client or prospect, when someone sends a referral your way, or when you meet someone interesting at a networking event. Mike Clemmons, at Bytecafe Consulting in Indiana, and Matt Moman, from Moman Sales in Florida, both echo the same sentiment. Customers, clients, and prospects want and need to be appreciated. Writing a quick note can easily achieve this and reinforce your business relationships.

A few things to remember when you write a personal note:

• Keep it short and to the point. A lengthy note is not necessary and may dilute the impact of the gesture.

• Be specific and sincere about the reason for writing your note. Make sure you mention at least one topic you talked about when you met. Remember, a generic handwritten note is no better than no note at all.

• Follow through if you promised something, such as a contact number or an introduction.

TIP #108
Go on a "listening tour" to learn what your clients need

When things slow down in your business, take some time to simply speak to your clients about their needs—without trying to sell them anything. You'll gain a lot of insight into what you can offer them in the future.

Case study: For three months when business slowed for her because of the recession, Paige Arnof-Fenn, owner of the Boston-based marketing company Mavens & Moguls, embarked on what she called a "listening tour." Instead of trying to sell a service she knew her clients couldn't afford, she met with as many prospects and influencers as she could for coffee, breakfast, lunch, or whatever. She said it wasn't that difficult to set up the meetings, especially when it was clear that this wasn't a sales call. The listening tour allowed Paige to talk to folks candidly about what problems they considered the most important to solve when budgets loosened up. Paige explained she was doing research, one-on-one, and asked a lot of open-ended questions that allowed them to share their hopes, dreams, and fears for their businesses.

The result? Just as soon as the market picked up again, Paige's phone started to ring with people wanting to follow up on the things they had discussed. Their budgets might have been smaller than she wanted, but Paige was signing up new clients for help in the very areas they'd discussed earlier.

Paige says that once her prospective clients talked through their concerns, they began to see how they could move forward. Also, since she'd done such a good job building relationships with her clients during the downturn, these same people thought of her first when things started to turn around!

TIP #109
Never say no to a potential customer

Never let your employees (or yourself for that matter) answer a customer or client's question with no.

No is a conversation ender, and what you *really* want are conversation extenders.

Case study: Recently while I was sitting in the reception area of Pilates on Fifth in New York, an exercise studio run by sisters Kimberly and Katherine Corp, a woman walked in and asked the receptionist, "Do you have yoga classes here?" Instead of saying "No, we don't," which would be the natural response since they didn't offer yoga, the receptionist responded, "We have Pilates and Cardiolates. Have you ever tried Cardiolates before?" This caught my attention because it was not the response I had expected and it was very clever.

The woman then asked what Cardiolates was and signed up for a class for the next day. By simply finding a way around saying no, the receptionist smartly recruited another client.

Scan to see a video

TIP #110
Find common interests with your customer

While many of us are taught that the first rule of sales is "Get your customer to like you," Robert Cialdini, author of *Influence: The Psychology of Persuasion*, told Frank Silverstein that this rule is missing the target. That should be the second rule of sales. The first rule of sales really should be: "Find something to like in your customer... and tell them."

When the customer recognizes that you like them, Cialdini says, everything changes. Your customer will start to like you too. They'll feel like you're going to look out for their best interests and they will be more open to saying yes to your requests.

How do you do that? How do you come to like someone when, in fact, you barely know them?

For starters, do an Internet search to read up on your customers, and look for common interests, experiences, or backgrounds. Or, ask a mutual acquaintance. If you both love to play tennis or went to the same college or have three kids, it gives you a chance to bring up something you'll both enjoy talking about.

If you don't have time to do this research, look around his or her office to see what reflects the core values that you have in common. You'll find it's much easier and nicer to do business with someone with whom you've developed a personal connection.

In addition, take a genuine interest in who they are and why they have come to you. Ask them what they need, and then try to present the features of your product or service that will best suit their needs. If it turns out you can't help them, it's OK to be honest with them. You might not make a sale right then, but you can be confident that when their needs change, or if they run into a friend who needs something that you do offer, they will surely recommend you, and/or be back to see you themselves.

TIP #111
Anticipate a nonpaying customer

When you're faced with a customer who is not paying up, you always want to be sure to have all of your ducks lined up in a row in case you end up having to sue them. Jack E. Kaufman, partner at the law firm Kaufman, Kaufman & Miller in Encino, California, gave us three things everyone should do when setting up a business relationship with someone new:

1. **Have your customer fill out a credit application.** Be certain they fill it out with their full and correct name (e.g., ABC Hardware Inc., not just ABC Hardware) and that it is signed by an owner or an officer of the company—not just an employee. Also, if possible, use a credit application that provides for a personal guarantee and has a provision for attorney fees and costs in the event you have to sue them. Finally, verify all of the information they provide—especially trade references, the length of their relationship, and payment history.

2. **Make sure your invoice has the correct name of the customer** (just like the credit application) and includes a statement that you are entitled to your attorney fees and cost of collection should the customer fail to pay. The invoice should also contain a fee for "carrying or servicing" the account—for example, "a service charge of (whatever the legal interest is in your state) will be made for invoices not paid within thirty days."

3. **Maintain a credit file.** This file should contain the customer's credit application, any correspondence between

the two of you (be sure to print out the e-mails), and a copy of a recent check they used for payment. If you have to sue your customer and collect a judgment, you will have the name and account number of their most recent bank. This information will be invaluable to your attorney in establishing your customer's obligation to pay you and will assist you in locating a source for payment.

TIP #112
Set time boundaries with your clients

Problem: Your clients feel that since they are paying you, you should be available to them twenty-four hours a day, seven days a week. Of course, you want to make sure they feel taken care of and you don't want them to jump ship to a competitor, but then again, you still want to have a personal life.

Solution: Establish your availability right at the outset of the relationship. Sterrin Bird, principal of Pacific Advancement Partners in San Francisco, has created a script that lets her clients know that she cares about them and that she will provide stellar service but that she also has limitations to her time.

She tells them, "I am one hundred percent committed to providing you excellent service. And to that end, when I am working on your project, I do not let any of my other clients encroach on your time. I also make this same promise to my other clients, so when I am working with them, I am one hundred percent focused on their needs. If it is an emergency, of course I am available to you, but if it is not, I like to give all my clients the focus they deserve."

In addition, in order to clearly send the message that she is not available when the workday is over, Sterrin never answers a client e-mail after business hours. She often reads her e-mails and even writes the responses, but she does not send them until business hours the next morning. Sending e-mails after hours only gives the message that you are available and open 24/7, and that is not the message some business owners want to convey.

TIP #113
Keep the "extras" in check

Problem: Your clients want you to throw in a lot of "extras" for free or for a highly reduced price.

Solution: Be aware that while it's fair for clients to ask for these freebies, it's also fair for you to answer with a no. In the long run, if you continue to give your clients your work for free, it will eat away at your core business. Don't do it.

Case study: Matt Bostock, founder of New York–based Lake 5 Media, which provides analytical software services for big media companies, says he occasionally receives requests from clients who want him to provide additional services without paying more. This type of work requires use of Lake 5's infrastructure and employees, both of which cost money. While Matt wants Lake 5 to be known as a company that provides excellent service, he is also incredibly mindful of the bottom line. Here's how he responds to these requests:

"While we would love to be able to provide you with this service, we'd have to charge you in order to do it correctly. If I gave it to you on the cheap, it wouldn't be sustainable and you would not get the kind of product you expect from us."

Matt says that time and time again, when it's explained in this way, his clients understand and it reinforces his company's reputation of delivering only top-notch products.

TIP #114
Use your customers as advisors

Customers are most likely your best source of product innovation, so use them.

Carol Roth, author of the book *The Entrepreneur Equation*, suggests creating a Customer Advisory Panel, or CAP, for your business. This panel should be made up of a diverse range of your best customers or clients whom you turn to for feedback in person or online (or both) regarding topics like product development, product launches, and customer service.

Not only will this CAP serve as an on-call focus group, but as your customers give their input, they'll have a more vested interest in your product or service and will more likely remain a customer as well as get the word out to their friends.

There's no need to pay these people—customers who like your company will generally be happy to help. But you could offer them some company swag (a T-shirt or tote bag) or a discount on a product or service you offer.

Extra tip: Abbie Schiller, founder of Los Angeles–based The Mother Company, took this concept one step farther and only worked with investors who were in her target demographic. Instead of taking a large chunk of start-up money from one angel investor, she decided to take small amounts from twenty moms and dads in her circle who loved her product. This group now serves as an informal advisory board, giving input on everything from product design to marketing.

Scan to see a video

TIP #115
Get your customers to help you improve your new products

When you launch a new product, no doubt you'll be wondering if the quality will be up to your customers' standards. Why not just ask them?

Josh Brookhart, managing director of TZG Partners in Shanghai, China, says that the best approach is to be honest with your customers—tell them emphatically right from the start that this is a new product launch and that while there may still be some issues, you promise to fix them right away—and then deliver on that promise with a short turnaround and a twenty-four-hour hotline.

Many customers will be happy to engage in the process of helping you improve and will feel a sense of pride in doing so (leading to a stronger connection with your company!). Take advantage of that help, and thank them in the process.

Being honest with your customers also takes the pressure off you to make your product totally perfect at launch. Of course, you should thoroughly test your products and make them the best they can be, but this gives you a little more margin for error.

How I use this: Fortunately for me, I received this tip from Josh a week before we were about to relaunch the entire GoodSearch site. Based on this advice, we rewrote our newsletter announcing the relaunch and included a paragraph asking all our users to participate in the process of making sure everything was working and easy to navigate. We received a bunch of e-mails from users thanking us for the new site and giving us some very helpful constructive criticism. They also nicely pointed out some inconsistencies we hadn't caught in our internal testing!

TIP #116
Use mistakes to engender loyalty

We all make mistakes. And at some point, we're going to annoy our customers because of them. In the spirit of making lemonade out of lemons, two different companies told us what they did to turn disasters into loyalty-creating events.

Case study 1: SkinnyScoop, based in the San Francisco Bay Area, is a company that makes it easy for women to create, share, and find the information they use to make decisions— and it's basically all online. So, as you can imagine, it was a bit of a disaster when their servers crashed for a few days and nobody could access the site.

Co-founder Eden Godsoe was very transparent about the server crash and created a contest where people were invited to answer the poll question "What do you do when you're having a down day?"—appealing to the universal experience of having everything go wrong. Anyone who answered won a SkinnyScoop T-shirt. Eden was overwhelmed (in a good way) by how many people sent supportive e-mails. And she now has hundreds of people marketing the brand by wearing their T-shirts across the country.

Case study 2: Los Angeles–based vitamin company Smarty-Pants posted a contest on Facebook offering a free bottle of vitamins to their three-hundredth fan. Co-founders Courtney Nichols and Gordon Gould found out after the fact that they couldn't tell who that was.

So, rather than fake it, they did the opposite. They outed themselves, admitted their mistake, and offered free bottles to the first twenty-five people to comment on how they screwed up. Not only did many of these fans then turn into customers, but they also shared the story with their friends, helping to expand the company's fan base on Facebook.

Mended fences are often stronger than those never tested at all.

Scan to see a video

TIP #117
Segment your customers into three categories

If you separate your customers into three basic categories—
A-list, B-list, and C-list—you can maximize and tailor your
service to meet their needs.

This goes against the mantra of "treat every customer as
though they were your only customer." While that's a nice
thought, it's impractical. In reality, not all customers mean
the same thing to your business and it's inefficient to treat
everyone exactly the same.

Brandon Hinkle from Chicago-based plura Financial
Solutions has worked out a way to divide everyone up:

- **The A-list** customers are those who take up the most
time but pay the most bills for you. They're strategically and
financially critical for your business.

- **The B-list** customers are those who you don't hear from
much and don't generate a ton of revenue for you—but they
pay on time and don't require a lot of resources.

- **The C-list** customers are the least profitable; they have
the lowest margins, smallest revenue, and require a lot of
attention. (They pay slowly, they're high-maintenance, and
they're not central to your bottom line.)

If you're doing a price increase, you may want to leave the
A's alone, raise the B's by a modest amount, and raise the C's
prices to the point where you're either happy with the profitability or they simply go away. This will free up more time
and cash to better serve your best customers.

Note: James Joy of Summit Service & Associates in Armonk, New York, figured out who his A, B, and C customers were by simply tracking the time his team spent on each customer and comparing it to the revenue they generated. It gave him a sense of the "true cost" of each of his clients.

TIP #118
Respond to negative customer feedback positively

The best way to win a customer for life is to make good on a mistake. But let's be honest, in the heat of the moment when someone is slamming you or your company, it's often hard to keep your emotions in check.

Stella Grizont, managing director of the entrepreneurial group Ladies Who Launch and founder of New York–based Woopaah, gives these steps for responding to an unhappy client:

1. **Thank the person for (a) taking the time and (b) sharing something uncomfortable:**

"Thank you for sharing this. I know it took time out of your schedule and we really appreciate the feedback."

This helps to immediately defuse what usually begins as a tense conversation.

2. **Acknowledge and repeat the way the customer feels:**

"I'm hearing that you're disappointed and frustrated."

What people care about most is being heard. So make that abundantly clear by using the same language they use.

3. **Cite what they see as the problem:**

"I understand that you said you ordered a size 6 and you said you received a size 8 and it came later than you expected."

State the problem according to how they see it (this isn't admitting to anything, this is just showing them that you're trying to step into their shoes). If you are able to do this, then they will be more open to whatever comes next. When you don't resist, it's difficult for someone to feel angry or frustrated.

4. Decide what you want to do with the feedback:

Choose whether you agree with the feedback and want to make amends or if you disagree. If you agree and want to make amends, offer an immediate solution and state it in a way that communicates your intention of keeping the customer:

"I'd like to send you a free pair as a sign of our desire to keep you as a loyal customer. We want to have you back and will do what it takes to make this right by you. It's not acceptable that we made a mistake with your order, and we will do everything we can to make sure it doesn't happen again."

If you disagree with the feedback or are not at fault, state that you disagree but understand.

"I realize this is how you're feeling and that you expected something else; however, we see on your receipt that this is indeed what you ordered."

or

"I accept this piece of feedback and thank you for sharing; however, I do disagree for these reasons... can you understand why I might see it this way?"

5. Create an honorable closure:

Thank them—again—for taking the time to share, and acknowledge that you have learned something of real value.

"Again, I appreciate your initiating this conversation. As we grow as a company, it's very useful to hear feedback, both good and bad, from our customers."

TIP #119
End customer interactions on a positive note

When you end an experience with a customer (whether it's at an event you're holding, after a service you've provided, or when they check out on your retail website), you want them to leave feeling positive about their experience with your company.

Karla Lightfoot, founder of New York City–based Hypno Happy, says the way she ensures people remember something good is to simply ask them, "What did you like most about your experience today?"

Important: If you simply ask customers "How did you like this experience?" and leave it open-ended, many people will tend to focus on the negative. But if you guide them to focus on something positive, it will help imprint a happy memory of their dealings with you. Studies show that endings are incredibly important in determining how we remember experiences.

TIP #120
Tap into social media data

Websites like Facebook will show you a calendar of upcoming birthdays. Why not take this information and use it?

Thomas Jandula, the CEO of Purpl Media in Hilton Head, South Carolina, says businesses can offer different premiums. For instance, restaurants can offer a free birthday meal, a hair salon can offer a haircut and blow-dry, and a liquor store can send a postcard for a complimentary bottle of wine. And this goes beyond birthdays—every minute of every day online social-media communities such as Facebook, Twitter, and LinkedIn generate enormous amounts of data. If your business has a presence on these sites (if you don't, you should!), this information can be a powerful asset that can easily make your small business stand out against the competition.

Case study: At John Huntington's California-based Long Beach Hydrobikes, his daughter and partner, Melissa Huntington, has developed a highly effective social-media tool. They rent out specially designed bicycles that ride on water, and when the happy customers return from their rides, Melissa snaps a photo which she posts in an album on their Facebook page. She takes the picture and tells them, "This is going to be on Facebook, so you can tag yourselves!" When they tag themselves on the Facebook picture, all their friends are notified that they were at Long Beach Hydrobikes. Melissa says it's free, it's fun, the customers love it, and they've received a ton of new Facebook "friends" that way.

Scan to see a video

TIP #121
Make your customer surveys count

It's incredibly easy to survey your customers using free online tools. But before you go out and start to ask questions, make sure you're asking them in a way that will result in useful answers. Dave Goldberg, the CEO of SurveyMonkey in Palo Alto, California, has a few tips on how to compose a meaningful survey:

1. **Avoid using "agree/disagree" answers.**

People have a tendency to be polite and agreeable, especially with researchers or people in positions of authority, which leads them to answer "agree" even if they don't totally mean it.

2. **Fully label and use the appropriate number of "scale points."**

Research shows that outcomes are more reliable when you use five- or seven-point scales.

A five-point example:

How interesting was the session? Please rate:

- ❑ Extremely interesting
- ❑ Very interesting
- ❑ Moderately interesting
- ❑ A little interesting
- ❑ Not at all interesting

A seven-point example:

Do you support or oppose a price change?

- ❑ Strongly support
- ❑ Moderately support

- ❑ Slightly support
- ❑ Neither support nor oppose
- ❑ Slightly oppose
- ❑ Moderately oppose
- ❑ Strongly oppose

3. **Choose the right words to make your questions clear, and be specific.**

For example:

Wrong way: *What did you think about the training session?*

Right way: *How engaging was the training session?*

- ❑ Extremely engaging
- ❑ Very engaging
- ❑ Moderately engaging
- ❑ Slightly engaging
- ❑ Not at all engaging

4. **Use words that have the same meaning for all of your respondents.**

Wrong way: *How cool did you think the company booth was?*

Right way: *How interesting was the company booth?*

5. **Avoid leading questions.**

Wrong way: *Did you think anything was awful at the event?*

Right way: *What did you like least about the event?*

TIP #122
Connect to customers with QR codes

If you still aren't sure what those funny square-looking graphics are throughout this book, go to page xv to learn more. If you know what they are and are intrigued to learn how you can use them for your small business, read on.

QR codes are a quick and efficient way to make a meaningful connection with a customer (or a reader). Hamilton Chan, the founder of Los Angeles–based Paperlinks (which created these QR codes for us), says the key to running a successful QR-code campaign is to make them relevant. The way you do this is by offering something special in exchange for the effort it takes to pull out a phone and scan the code. To help get a customer interested in scanning the code, make sure there is some kind of call to action in order to make it worth their while. For instance, "Scan the code and get a 20 percent discount on your purchase today," or "For additional information on how our custom-made furniture is constructed, scan here." Another way to use a QR code is to place it in the window of a store to snag a customer walking by. This code can alert them to a sale going on, or allow them to make a reservation at a restaurant or an appointment at a salon after hours. It also is an opportunity for a customer to become more familiar with your brand. Your QR code can lead to a landing page that takes customers directly to your Facebook page, a newsletter, or encourages them to leave their e-mail so they can be notified about special offers and sales.

You can also track the number of people who scan your QR codes, which can provide a lot of interesting customer data for you to use to plan new promotions.

You can see we are big fans of QR codes ourselves, and that's why we've placed them in the book. Our intention was to enhance the reader experience by linking readers to relevant videos that give more information on the tip itself or on the company that's profiled in the tip.

Scan to see a video

TIP #123
Get your holiday gift noticed

There really is no rule that says Christmas is the only time to send out gifts! If you're going to put the effort into making a statement, Rieva Lesonsky, founder of GrowBiz Media in Lakewood, California, suggests sending out your business holiday presents right before Thanksgiving. That way, your gift will arrive early and will be remembered longer.

People are inundated with presents from work-related people at the holidays. For instance, in one day last year, I got a margarita basket, a big box of brownies, a bottle of wine, a box of chocolates, a flower arrangement, and a bonsai tree!

I consider myself to be lucky (albeit on the way to major weight gain) to receive so many wonderful gifts during the holidays. But after sending a quick thank-you note, I admittedly don't always remember who sent what. That's a shame—because if you are going to spend money giving your clients gifts, you certainly want them to remember it!

Following up: The Los Angeles–based company Woven, with whom GoodSearch shared an office for a while, follows this same idea with their holiday party. They hold it *before* Thanksgiving instead of later in the year so that all of their clients are sure to be able to come!

TIP #124
Answer the phone

It is incredibly annoying and a real turnoff to call a company, especially during work hours, and get an answering machine. Among other things, it gives the perception that your company is relatively unconcerned with providing top-notch customer service. So, whenever possible, make sure your customers don't have this experience.

Mark Eshman, the cofounder of Sun Valley, Idaho–based ClearRock Capital, has solved this problem in his company by giving every phone in the office access to the main line. Yes, there is one person primarily responsible for answering the phone, but if he is busy, any other employee can pick up the phone as well.

Watch out! There is one big risk to this policy. While voice mail might be irritating to your customers, talking to an unprofessional or awkward employee could be much worse. As such, if you are going to ask your employees to answer the main line, you also have to train them on how to deal with calls. At GoodSearch, we have told our employees that if the caller's question goes beyond their expertise, they should simply take a message and immediately pass the message along to someone who can handle the request. We then have a strict policy that the person must be called back within five minutes.

TIP #125
Don't give away professional advice for free

Problem: If you're in a service business, chances are you get a lot of friends and acquaintances asking for your advice for free. For instance, I am quite guilty of calling my uncle whenever I have a legal question (sorry, Uncle Jack!). If you're like my uncle, you may be happy to give this advice for free to your friends (or nieces), but you don't want to be giving away your expertise to prospective clients.

In fact, the last thing you want to do is develop a reputation for being too free with your hard-earned knowledge, because then people around you may actually stop valuing it. So how do you politely convert those advice seekers into clients?

Solution: Robert Livingstone, founder of West Palm Beach–based Ideal Cost, has come up with a few polite responses for when he feels someone is trying to pick his brain for free:

- "Yes, I can surely solve your problem. When would you like to schedule a client meeting?"
- "That's a great question. I'd be more than happy to answer it, but I don't know if I already gave you my hourly rate or not. In either case it is _____ dollars an hour."
- "I'd love to help you out, but it wouldn't be fair to take time away from my paying clients right now. Would you like to engage us for services?"
- "I can be of help, but I assume you know that this is my job and how I support my family. Should we compare schedules to set up a time to talk?"

TIP #126
Let customers know you listened to them

When you get customer feedback and then act upon it, be sure to follow up with that customer and let them know that you made changes based on their suggestions—even if it's months later. This can be just a quick e-mail saying, "I just wanted to let you know that because of your suggestion we have (and then detail what the change is)." This takes only a couple of minutes, but generally results in increased loyalty from customers—even those who initially were complaining about your service!

How I use this: At GoodSearch we had a number of complaints from people who were unhappy with a change we made with the layout of our site. We took the feedback to heart and decided to modify it. Because of a long list of more pressing items we had to get done, we were not able to make the change for a week. But I then e-mailed all of the people who initially wrote to us to let them know that because of their helpful feedback, we had improved the site.

The responses I received were, across the board, enthusiastic. From "Thank you so much for telling me. I never expected to hear from you again," to "I can't believe there is a real person reading these e-mails and listening to the suggestions. I'm going to tell everyone I know about GoodSearch!"

Important: Don't forget to share customer feedback with your employees. While the customer service team gets to feel good about reading an e-mail saying, "I love your service," Wharton School lecturer Lawrence Gelburd says it's important to make sure everyone else on the team sees the results of their collective hard work too. It makes them proud of the job they're doing, keeps them in touch with the end user, and serves as a great motivational tool. So, every once in a while, compile these e-mails and send them around to everyone in your office or read them at a staff meeting.

TIP #127
Reduce your no-shows

Problem: Customers make appointments and reservations at your company but then never show up.

Solution: Simply ask people to give their credit card information when they make their reservations and tell them there's a cancellation fee for no-shows.

Case study: John Huntington of Long Beach Hydrobikes in Long Beach, California, rents out water bicycles and says that he has sometimes turned away customers at the door when all his bikes have been reserved ahead of time, only to have the reservations never show up. "It breaks your heart in this tough economy to lose business like that."

John now takes credit card information and explains his cancellation-fee policy when someone makes a reservation. The truth is, he says, you don't even have to write down the credit card info. The mere threat of a charge, he's found, is more than enough to ensure that they will call up and cancel if they can't make it. In the very rare cases where they don't show up, he's decided it creates too much bad will to actually charge the fees and he just absorbs that cost—it's the threat that keeps most people honest.

TIP #128
Fire your customers

Once a year, give the boot to 20 percent of your customers. Does that sound crazy to you? According to Les McKeown, founder of the company Predictable Success in Marblehead, Massachusetts, getting rid of a fifth of your customers each year is the only way to grow.

Here is his reasoning. Most companies follow the Pareto principle (otherwise known as the 80-20 rule), meaning that 80 percent of their business comes from 20 percent of their clients. That means that companies are spending a lot of time on a lot on customers who aren't bringing in significant revenue. In addition, it's these "small potato" customers who are frequently the most high-maintenance, which means that they could be taking up more of your resources than they're worth. In other words, those are resources you could be spending on servicing your higher-paying clients or recruiting new clients.

Here is how Les does it. At the end of every year, he takes an inventory and finds out who the bottom 20 percent of his customers are. He then sets up a meeting or a call and says to them very nicely, "I've really enjoyed working with you and I sincerely thank you so much for your business, but moving forward, I feel that I'm not in a position to be the best resource for you. I do know someone who specializes in your needs and I've spoken to them and they're excited to meet with you." The key, Les says, is giving them a referral so that you don't engender any ill will. And referring a customer to someone else in your industry will build some goodwill among others in your field as well.

Tip: Marley Majcher, CEO of the Los Angeles–based The Party Goddess!, has had to fire a number of customers and says she always writes herself a "script" to follow when she has to have that kind of conversation. Unproductive customers are often very convincing (which is why you started working with them in the first place), and having the script allows her to stick to her guns, keep her emotions in check, and ensures she doesn't say something she'll regret later!

Watch out! I know it can be scary to fire a customer, because that means losing revenue. But Les McKeown says it's a risk that will pay off. Let's assume you ditch, say, five clients or customers whom you spend two hours each a week servicing but who are a pain in the neck and cost you money. As a result you now have ten hours to work on your top 20 percent of clients who love you, aren't a chronic pain, and who may be prepared to pay you for additional services.

CHAPTER EIGHT

GETTING YOUR MESSAGE OUT THERE

Marketing your company and courting the press

TIP #129	Don't rush your news to the media	190
TIP #130	When it comes to social media, be strategically social	191
TIP #131	Getting a handle on SEO (Search Engine Optimization)	194
TIP #132	Get celebrities to use your product	196
TIP #133	Entice the media	197
TIP #134	Have your photo taken	199
TIP #135	Market your company by marketing yourself	200
TIP #136	Create a personal story to connect with customers	201
TIP #137	Collect testimonials from real people	203
TIP #138	Ask for video testimonials	204
TIP #139	Take your product to the streets	205
TIP #140	Five-mile rule	206
TIP #141	Event Planning 101	208

TIP #142 Compete with the big-box stores   210

TIP #143 Share your marketing costs   211

TIP #144 Partner with people who reach a
              similar audience   212

TIP #145 Make all your marketing materials
              do triple duty   213

TIP #146 Determine your company's personality   214

TIP #129
Don't rush your news to the media

Never send a press release the same day you launch a new product or service.

It's tempting to do this when you have an exciting new product or service you want to tell the world about. But wait! Take a cue from Broadway, which always has preview performances *before* opening night. Launch your product or site first and let it be tested out in the real world so that you can get all the kinks ironed out before you let the media know about it.

The last thing you want to have happen is to get a big story, draw a lot of people to your store or to your site, and then have something go wrong! Or, just as bad, you don't want a reporter to call you or visit you and then have your product or site be less than perfect—that's the last thing you want them to write about.

So launch your site or new product in "beta" first. In essence, take it out for a test drive. Once you know it's really good to go, send out your release!

TIP #130
When it comes to social media, be strategically social

When taking your business into the social-media realm, be strategic about your messaging.

Deb Armstrong of Empower Consulting Group says you should align your status updates with your overall marketing goals so you can build a rapport, establish a relationship, and learn what your customers want.

It is always much easier to fill a need when you know exactly what that need is without making assumptions. For example, let's say the XYZ Real Estate Company is trying to use social media to set themselves apart from their competition by becoming the "trusted expert" in selling homes. They offer their expertise with information that a home seller would find interesting or helpful. By having the answers, and demonstrating they have a great deal of knowledge, their clients know whom to call when they need help selling their home.

Here's how to do it:

Sample Facebook Status Update #1:
Need some advice on how to stage your home to achieve maximum sale price? In this new how-to video, our resident expert shares some valuable yet easy tips for you. Do you have any suggestions to add?

Comment from fan:
I've always been a huge proponent of staging—my favorite tip is to bake cookies just before an open house. It gives the home that comfortable family feeling.

Response to fan comment:
Thank you for sharing! We love the fresh-baked cookie aroma as well! Another suggestion along that line,

which doesn't require cooking, is to pick up a scented candle at Pier 1—that will also do the trick!

Sample status update #2:

Most people know that homeownership comes with great tax breaks. Know what you can and can't deduct as a home owner with this video from our local tax expert. Don will be answering your questions here.

Comment from fan:

The video talks a little about home improvements. Can those be deducted every year?

Response to fan comment:

You will always want to contact your tax attorney regarding those specific questions, but generally speaking, home improvements are factored in during the sale of the home and not at the time of the improvement, unless they are the same, of course.

Heather Lopez, founder of Heather Lopez Enterprises, agrees that social media is all about making it clear that you are an expert on something and making yourself part of the conversation. In short, if you have something interesting to say, people are going to want to hear it. But if all you're doing is talking about what you have to sell, chances are people will begin to tune out.

Here's an example: If you are a children's retailer, here are two items you could tweet about:

1. We have a great new selection of baby clothes
2. Ten surefire tips to get stains out of baby clothing

While the first tweet certainly gets right to the point and talks directly about a revenue generating opportunity, the second message will likely generate more revenue. Both ideas are reaching people who care about baby clothes, but one, in essence, asks for money while the other one is a conversation piece. The article about getting stains out is much more likely to be passed along, bringing new customers to your site (and, on the site, you can then market the new selection of clothes!).

TIP #131
Getting a handle on SEO (Search Engine Optimization)

Search engine marketing is incredibly important to your business. Why? Well, if you're a high-end tailor in Durham, North Carolina, then you want to make sure that when someone does a search for "high-end tailor Durham" on a search engine, your business comes up within the top few choices.

One way to ensure that this happens is to pay for advertising on particular search terms. But another way is to create your site in a way that the search engines list you first. Search engine optimization (SEO) is an evolving medium that requires commitment and resources just like any ongoing project. It's also not something that you, or anyone you hire, are going to master in an hour. But according to small business consultant John Chao, it's something that you can easily learn over time from numerous sources on the Web if you're willing to put in the effort. Simply do a search for "SEO tips" and you'll find pretty much all you need to know. It just takes time.

If you don't have the time or inclination to learn SEO yourself, and you do want to hire a consultant, John says there are some factors to evaluate: First, as with any consulting firm, talk to the person who will be managing your account, not the salesperson or senior manager. Second, ask for references and follow up (be sure to ask those clients what the shortcomings of the SEO firm are—nobody's perfect). Third, ask to see case studies of their clients in your industry. SEO is not one-size-fits-all and should be customized, depending on the focus of your site. Make sure you choose a firm that has expertise in your style of website, whether it be informational, e-commerce, education, or B2B.

In addition, if you concentrate on your user experience, the higher SEO results should follow. The more people like your site, the more people will visit it and link to it, all of which brings it up higher in the search results.

John also warns that once you hire the firm, you do not have license to sit back and stop paying attention. As with most consultants, you get out what you put in. And it's your brand so make sure the company is not employing any "black-hat tactics" (such as paying for backlinks from other sites) that, if discovered, will be looked upon unkindly by the search engines. In 2011, Google penalized J. C. Penney and lowered its rankings in the search results in reaction to some tactics used by their SEO consultant on their behalf. If it can happen to J. C. Penney, it can happen to you.

TIP #132
Get celebrities to use your product

A photo of an A-list celebrity holding your product is the Holy Grail for many companies. But let's face it, it's nearly impossible to get.

Los Angeles–based Solas Fashion founder Kara Kurcz has figured out how to do it. Her bags have been featured in everything from gossip magazines to the *Today* show and have been used by Carrie Underwood, Cameron Diaz, Fergie, and many others. Here's her trick: Instead of contacting the celebrities themselves, Kara reaches out to the places they shop.

Each week, she buys copies of *Us Weekly*, *People*, and *In Touch* and she makes a note every time one of the magazines mentions a store a celebrity shopped at—especially the ones that are not in LA or New York and probably have fewer companies trying to get them to carry their products. She then calls the store directly to try to persuade them to sell her bag. Once her products are in these stores, she knows they'll be seen by the right people.

Kara also found a way to get her product placed on trendy television shows. She watches the shows that twenty-somethings watch and writes down the name of the costume designers listed in the credits at the end of the program. By contacting these people, she was able to get her product featured on *The O.C.*—the perfect show to market a trendy handbag!

Scan to see a video

TIP #133
Entice the media

When you pitch a story to a reporter, try to see your story from their perspective. You'll be much more successful in piquing their interest.

The first step is getting the reporter on the phone. You'll be surprised how many really do answer their phones when you call. The hard part is getting them engaged once you've got their attention.

Secondly, you have to be creative when you pitch your story. Think elevator pitch over the phone. Remember, most reporters are not interested in your company per se and are very busy. What *will* interest them, however, is how your company's story fits into what else is happening in the world, or how your company fits into a news event that's coming up. Keep in mind that news is much more than covering wars and disasters. For example, holidays such as Valentine's Day and Thanksgiving are also considered news events, so if you can, give your story a Valentine's twist and pitch it in early February. Finally, take time to read the reporter's recent stories. You need to get a sense of what each reporter typically writes about, and then craft your pitch to fit his or her interests.

Case study: On *Your Business*, we get pitched every single day, as you can imagine, by companies who want to be profiled on the show. Recently, the founder of one company called me and told me all about her product, which was a children's video. As a mom, I appreciated the product, but from the perspective of our show, her story didn't fit in. Just because she owns a small business and we broadcast stories about small business doesn't mean her story is appropriate for us. If she had looked carefully at our format, she would have noticed that our business stories focus on a business lesson and that we explain those lessons by telling the stories of individual companies.

Through an odd coincidence, I ran into this founder several months later. As we talked about her business, she told me how she'd turned down venture-capital money and funded her company by reaching out to moms in her neighborhood. Now, that was just the kind of story our viewers love, and we ended up featuring her efforts to find funding as a story on our broadcast.

Bottom line: If she had better understood what we look for when she first spoke to me, she might have been more successful with her pitch the first time around.

Scan to see a video

TIP #134
Have your photo taken

Make sure to have a series of professional-looking photos of yourself, your staff, your products, and your office space. If you don't want to spend the money on a professional photographer, that's OK as long as the photos look good. In most cases, just a few high-resolution photos taken with a decent point-and-shoot digital camera can do the trick.

Why? Rod Kurtz, executive editor of the *Huffington Post* "Small Business" section, says that even the biggest news organizations rarely send a photographer when they write about you these days. He has had stories held up more times than he can count because the company he's profiling couldn't get him any photos. If you have photos ready to go, the process runs that much more smoothly.

TIP #135
Market your company by marketing yourself

Every time you give a speech, you're getting your company's name out there—this helps you get customers, partnerships, employees, and if you're in the market, perhaps even an interested acquirer. So how do you start? Who's going to ask you to speak? Shari Boyer, CEO of the Los Angeles–based cause-marketing company Good Solutions Group, explains what you need in order to craft your pitch:

- **Develop several abstracts:** Write descriptions of topics that are timely, appealing, and demonstrate your expertise.

- **Update your bio:** Make certain it positions you as an authority in your field and includes a professional headshot.

- **Research opportunities:** Start with regional business organizations, alumni groups, or local chapters of national and international industry organizations that meet regularly. Chances are you may already be a member of one such group, which gives you an advantage.

- **Partner with a colleague or two:** Sometimes it's easier to pitch a panel discussion with several viewpoints than just a solo presentation.

- **Pitch with knowledge:** Before contacting the appropriate organization, know the basics about the speaking opportunity, such as booking lead-time, length of speech, and previous speakers/topics, to make sure you're on target.

- **Have a video:** It's helpful to have a prepackaged video of yourself speaking on your subject, whether you're speaking just to the camera or from a previous engagement.

TIP #136
Create a personal story to connect with customers

How do you make your company stand out in a saturated market where everyone is providing a similar service or product? For example, there may be five nail salons within a couple of blocks of the one you just opened and most customers don't know what differentiates one from another.

Often a real, personal connection or shared values with the owner of the business will bring the customer back. Charlena Miller, a marketing consultant from Portland, Oregon, says sharing your authentic story is a good vehicle for making that connection. But for your story to be most effective, it should have two key elements:

<u>Part A:</u> What inspired you to start this company?

The first part of the story should talk about your *passion* for your work. Why did you pick this business? Is it a family business? A hobby? A talent? Something you came to in order to answer a personal problem? Why is your work special to you?

<u>Part B:</u> What difference do you hope to make in other people's lives?

The second part of the story should talk about *your customers*. What do you want them to experience? Are you saving them time? Are you making them feel better about themselves and helping them enjoy life more? What are the customers' needs that you are meeting?

Once you have answered those questions, you can craft your story by mixing the best parts of each. One note of caution: While people are interested in your "short story," they may not be interested in your "novel." So try your story out on a couple of friends, as well as potential or current customers, to make sure it's compelling before putting it out there for the world!

Case study: Mark Bitterman and Jennifer Turner Bitterman opened a small shop in Portland, Oregon, featuring hundreds of different varieties of local and imported handmade salt costing many times the price of salt sold in supermarkets. One of the key factors in their success is that they created a story that distinguishes their products from everything else on the market. Mark tells how he discovered his first artisanal salt at a roadside café while motorcycling through northern France at the age of twenty. He had a steak seasoned with traditional French handmade sea salt, and the flavor was so life changing that it prompted him to begin seeking out and collecting regionally made salts from around the world. When he opened his shop, his goal was to share these exotic flavors gathered from places as remote as Tibet, Morocco, Hawaii, Peru, Djibouti, and Bali. He even wrote a book on salt explaining its history and offering regional recipes featuring these unusual salts.

Mark's story transformed an ordinary kitchen staple into a romantic adventure. Who wouldn't want to be a part of that?

Scan to see a video

TIP #137
Collect testimonials from real people

Is it better to have a testimonial from a celebrity or from someone who is more like your customer? Well, it depends. Steve Martin (not *that* Steve Martin!), the UK director of Influence At Work, says people follow the lead of others who are similar to them. And the more friends who make the same suggestion, the more likely we are to follow.

Thus, if we see our friends behaving in a certain way, we are more likely to do the same. If everyone we know is talking about a certain restaurant in town, we're more likely to go there ourselves.

Bottom line: A testimonial from a movie star might get people's attention, but it's the opinions of people who are most like ourselves that will actually attract us to be new customers. This is why word of mouth and social-media sites can be so important to advertising your business.

TIP #138
Ask for video testimonials

If you have a product that lends itself to a colorful experience, encourage your customers to upload videos of themselves using it. It's true that a picture is worth a thousand words, and there is no better testimonial than seeing real customers enjoying your products.

Case study: San Francisco–based Gyrobike makes a cool device that replaces the front wheel of your child's bicycle to make it easy to learn how to ride. What parent doesn't want to take a video of their child's first ride and share it? Knowing this, Gyrobike's Ashleigh Harris includes an invitation in each box that encourages parents to take that video and then upload the footage to YouTube. When parents send the company the link to the video, she sends them a T-shirt as a thank-you.

Does it work? The simple invitation to upload the video has resulted in more than half a million views on the company's dedicated YouTube channel. Marketing does not get more authentic than that!

People love to share things about their kids, themselves, their companies, you name it—so encourage and reward them for doing it about your products!

TIP #139
Take your product to the streets

Find out where and when the influencers among your potential customers convene, and hand something out to them.

Case study: Anticipating the next big product launch from Apple, Craig Dalton, co-founder of DODOcase in San Francisco, developed an iPad case that resembles an old-fashioned bound book. In order to sell it, he needed to get people to start talking about it. He had to find a way to get to the most fanatic Apple fans.

The day Apple launched the iPad, he enlisted a group of brand ambassadors to hand out flyers to people waiting in line at the Apple store. Each of these ambassadors received a ten-dollar commission for every DODOcase that was bought by someone with whom they had contact.

Did it work? The total cost of this campaign was $500, but it netted more than $15,000 in DODOcase sales in those first few days. And, just as important, those Apple fanatics became DODOcase fans, sharing their find on social-media sites. One of the people in line that day turned out to be a prominent blogger, who helped put DODOcase on the map.

TIP #140
Five-mile rule

When it comes to marketing your local business, keep focused on a *five-mile radius.*

Linda Duke, of Duke Marketing in San Rafael, California, says the best piece of advice she can give any retailer, restaurant operator, or other type of main-street business owner is to engage in local-store marketing—focus on the area within a ten-minute drive of your business. Neighborhood marketing is a community-based strategy and, best yet, the cost is nominal.

Here's how to do it:

Empower your employees to be ambassadors.

Remember that your staff can be your best marketers. Give them samples of your products or coupons to share with their friends. Make sure they fully understand the best selling points of your company. And treat them well. Happy employees are likely to spread the word about your business. Alternatively, if someone is upset at the way they're treated at work, they'll be sure to tell their friends, and the bad word of mouth will end up costing you customers.

Community partnerships

Examine your target demographic and partner with organizations that interact with those consumers. Are you trying to attract families? Support the Girl Scouts, sponsor a local sports team, or participate in a school fundraiser. Do you want business professionals to visit your business? Get involved with the local chamber of commerce. Partnering with these types of organizations will send a message to the community that you're a good corporate neighbor.

Local PR

Combining local store marketing efforts with public relations is a cost-effective way of getting your message out to the community. Get to know the editor of your local newspaper and send press releases with photos when you have something new to share. For instance, let's say you own the local gym and you find out the food pantry is running low on canned goods. You can challenge your members (who are trying to get fit and lose weight) to donate two hundred pounds of food by the end of the month. When you reach the goal, take a photo of your members and the donated cans of food on a scale and send it off to the local paper. There is a good chance the story will get a write-up in the local paper, and the goodwill from helping the food pantry is far more credible and less expensive than spending dollars on advertising about your gym.

TIP #141
Event Planning 101

If you're going to spend the time and expense to plan an event, don't make a rookie mistake that turns it into a disaster. Wendy Silverstein of WS&A Communications in New York shared a few of her best ideas to keep in mind when planning your next event:

• Check your industry calendar and make sure there's not another big event going on the same day! If there's no way around it, you might consider holding your event in the same neighborhood as the other event. That way, you can leverage the other event to help boost participation in yours.

• Electronic invites look just as nice as the real ones— don't bother sending paper. And always send an e-mail reminder the day before the event.

• If you rent a space, make sure the doors and elevator can accommodate anything you need to bring in.

• New and interesting spaces that people have not frequented before can create a buzz. It could be a restaurant, museum, or private club. And new spaces are often more affordable than established ones. Many times, event-space operators represent more than one locale. It's always good to ask. In fact, they may be able to offer another venue if your first choice is beyond your budget.

• An engaging speaker, a wine tasting, or a top local chef preparing food can be a big draw if you want to get people to your event. If you are hosting an event away from your home turf, it can be helpful to have an insider in that locale who will partner with you (and invite their contacts).

• If you really want someone special to show up, offer a car service—people are less likely to cancel if they are expecting a car!

• Make sure there is a run-of-show timeline. Think of pacing, e.g., what happens when guests arrive, how long should cocktails be, who will be speaking, when do things need to wrap up? There should be someone keeping an eye on the clock, so they can move things along as needed.

• If you are planning to hand out goody bags, keep them tucked away until the event is well under way. Make sure your company branding is clearly identified and that anything you give away is not going to break—which could be embarrassing.

• By all means, be ready with a few extra place settings and extra goody bags just in case an unexpected VIP shows up at the door.

TIP #142
Compete with the big-box stores

Underprice them. Yes, you heard me right. Charge *less* for your products than they do.

But here's the catch—don't do it all of the time. As a small business owner, you certainly can't charge less for your products than, let's say, Walmart, which has enormous purchasing power that you don't. But you can beat them on price for an item or two for, as an example, three hours on a Saturday.

That's what veteran small business salesman and consultant Tom Egelhoff, owner of Bozeman, Montana–based Smalltownmarketing.com, says. If you make your offer splashy enough, you can draw people into your store—and then get them to return by wowing them with your attention to customer service, your convenient location, your smaller size, and the other intangible but important competitive advantages you have over a big-box store.

Tip: The cost of this promotion can be shared with your suppliers. Ask them for a good deal on a limited supply of their product. It may be worth it for them as a way to market their product as well.

TIP #143
Share your marketing costs

Wholesalers and distributors often have co-op advertising funds that they can use to buy ad space in conjunction with your business.

Steve Strauss, author of *The Small Business Bible*, remembers a billboard his father, the founder of California-based Carpet World, had along the San Diego Freeway. The billboard said, "Elegance Underfoot—Carpet World," and in the corner it said, "featuring Ban-Lon Carpets." This was a win-win situation: Ban-Lon got major visibility and Carpet World got a full billboard for half the price.

How I use this: At GoodSearch I have used this technique on a much smaller scale. We once held a contest for our users and asked one of our partner retailers to supply the prize. The national bookseller Barnes & Noble gave us a Nook to give away to the winner. We had a great prize and B&N received some valuable free marketing for a new product they were trying to push.

TIP #144
Partner with people who reach a similar audience

The easiest, cheapest way to gain exposure is to do an exchange with someone who is reaching a similar target group.

Case study 1: Lea Richards, owner of the mail-order barbeque business Pig of the Month BBQ in Dayton, Ohio, teamed up with a grilling-accessory company to exchange coupons. Whenever they received an order, they'd put a "Pig of the Month" coupon in the customer's box along with their materials. And Lea did the same for them.

Case study 2: Lindsay Lopez, owner of Form Pilates in New York City, partners with other businesses to hold events. They both publicize the event so that each of their audiences is introduced to the other's products. In addition, it makes the event much cheaper. For example, Lindsay held a wine-tasting session with a local wine store and a tea tasting with a tea store soon after. Through these events, Lindsay met new potential clients and turned her Pilates studio from just a place to work out into a real community presence.

How I use this: At GoodSearch we did an exchange with the company Network for Good, which also speaks to nonprofits and people who support nonprofits. They put a message in our newsletter and we put one in theirs. The wonderful thing about this was that it was an exchange between two like-minded companies speaking to the same type of people. We did not have to get into a long negotiation or marketing discussion. I like what they do and they like what we do, so we helped each other out.

TIP #145
Make all your marketing materials do triple duty

One way to make your marketing money go farther is to follow the *three-times rule*. If you are going to buy something, make sure you can use it for three different purposes.

Angela Jia Kim, owner of Om Aroma and Savor the Success business network for women entrepreneurs in New York City, uses this rule with all of her marketing collateral. For example, she printed a postcard for her store but made sure the way it was designed and written would allow it to be used as a business card, as a card she could hand out in the store, and a piece of direct mail.

She took the same approach when she bought containers to use for packaging her "caviar eye creams." She carefully chose a size and design that could also be used to package "travel size" and sample containers for some of her other products.

How I use this: Whenever I spend money on printing a nice piece of marketing material, I try to keep the information general enough so it can be used in multiple places.

I learned this the hard way when I printed up two different brochures, one for a PTA convention and a different one for the Association of Fundraising Professionals convention. The brochures were identical except that one said "school" and the other said "charity." When I ran out of the ones that said "charity," I couldn't use the leftover "school" ones. It would have made much more sense to just have one design that said "charity or school," which is what we do now.

TIP #146
Determine your company's personality

Problem: You're having trouble coming up with breakthrough marketing communications because you're not entirely sure about the voice your company's brand should have.

Solution: Gather your team and ask yourselves, "If this company were a person, who would it be?" Ben Nemo, the founder of Scorpio Ventures in Atlanta, says that it's much easier for people to understand characters than it is to understand companies. So once you've determined that your company is a "suave Don Juan," or a "frat-house beer-pong champion," it's much easier to design consistent, impactful marketing communications around that character.

Watch out! Ben says be careful when you're doing this exercise not to use generalizations. For example, a "cool person" can mean different things to different people, but a "Fifth Avenue socialite" is much more specific and commonly understood.

CHAPTER NINE

BUILDING RELATIONSHIPS

Networking and communication

TIP #147   Be the first one at every event   216

TIP #148   Arm people with specific ways to help you   218

TIP #149   Earn business credibility by being an ongoing presence   220

TIP #150   Make friends with your neighbors   221

TIP #151   Meet people face-to-face   222

TIP #152   Creatively contact companies you want to work with   224

TIP #153   Meet new people every week   225

TIP #154   Follow up after you meet someone   226

TIP #155   Find new leads in your old contacts   228

TIP #156   Tap your network to stay on top of trends   229

TIP #157   Leave the perfect voice mail message— incoming and outgoing   230

TIP #158   Write the perfect cold e-mail   232

TIP #159   Attend conferences for free   233

TIP #160   Turn your inexperience into an asset   234

TIP #147
Be the first one at every event

Problem: You're invited to an event where there will be a lot of potential investors (or customers or marketing partners...), but you are a little shy and you are terrible at networking. Your instinct may be to arrive late so you're not the first awkward person there.

Solution: Arrive exactly on time.

It may seem a bit uncomfortable to be one of the first people at a party, but in reality, being one of those early birds makes it much easier to break the ice with the other early birds before everyone settles into little groups. Colleen DeBaise, the special projects editor for *Entrepreneur* magazine who pointed this out to us, says it's hard to break into a group of strangers who are already mid-conversation. It's much easier when there are just a few people all feeling a bit awkward and you're almost forced into a conversation with the other early arrivers.

How I use this: Though most people wouldn't assume that I'm shy, I do have my moments...and I've certainly spent a lot of time pretending to write a "very important e-mail" at the side of the room while really I'm just covering up for the fact that I can't find anyone to talk to. What a waste of time! I'm much better starting a conversation with someone standing alone than navigating my way into a group of people I don't know.

Suggestion 1: For people who are not very good at starting conversations, Eric Kaufman, a partner at Premier Sports & Entertainment, who has made a career out of being outgoing, told us that the best "pick-up line" at a networking event is the "no-pick-up, pick-up line." He says, simply go up to someone and say, "Hi, I'm <<Enter your name here>>." Eric says you shouldn't overthink it. Just walk up and say hello. While you may get a few cold shoulders, most people are nice, and just introducing yourself is the best icebreaker.

Suggestion 2: If you are shy or just don't feel comfortable walking into a place where you don't know anyone, make it easy on yourself. Call ahead and talk to the president or membership person. Tell them you are new to the event and ask if they would have someone meet you at the registration table and take you around to meet a few of the key members to get you started.

TIP #148
Arm people with specific ways to help you

When someone in a position to help you truly expresses excitement about your business, take advantage of it. But keep in mind, simple enthusiasm won't advance your cause. It's up to you to turn that excitement into something that's actually productive.

Justine Stamen Arrillaga, founder of New York–based nonprofit the TEAK Fellowship, says that when she meets someone who wants to help, she always asks for one of three very specific items—products, services, or favors—that can help her business. Being specific about what is needed accomplishes the following: (a) the person making the offer doesn't have to read your mind—instead they can focus their attention on getting you what you need; (b) you are sure to get something you actually want instead of having to turn down a nice offer of something you never wanted in the first place; and (c) giving them three items increases the chances that they will really be able to fulfill at least one of your requests.

My experience: When I go on speaking engagements, after the program I am often asked by people in the audience for help with their business. Here are two different approaches:

Ineffective: I am just launching my T-shirt company and would love to get your help. Here is my website. Please take a look at it and tell me what you think.

Effective: I am just about to launch my T-shirt company. I believe this would make a great story for the *Wall Street Journal* "Small Business" section. I know that the editor is on your show a lot. Would it be possible for you to send her my story pitch? If you're not comfortable with doing that, I understand. In that case, would you be willing to look over my press release to let me know if you have any suggestions?

While it may feel awkward to ask a stranger for help, don't forget that often people are flattered if you ask for their advice. Just be tactful about it, and remember, it never hurts to try.

TIP #149
Earn business credibility by being an ongoing presence

Every industry holds a number of events. Keep going to them and eventually you'll end up knowing everyone. The first time you go to something, you may feel like a complete outsider. But once you've attended a few times, you'll suddenly be seen as an insider. Ramon Ray, editor of Smallbiztechnology .com, says it simply takes showing up.

Why is this important? Through these events, you will get to know the key influencers in your industry or community. While at the event, you should share information, connect people to each other, and be friendly. Gradually you'll become the person everyone wants to meet. This is a smart and effective way to gain visibility, trust, and credibility.

Here's the payoff: Melinda Emerson, known as "Small-BizLady" and editor of Succeedasyourownboss.com, who runs the very popular #SmallBizChat on Twitter, says the best way to position yourself as a thought leader in your industry is to position yourself as the convener. In other words, be a connector. Host small dinners where people have the opportunity to network with each other, create tweet chats where people can learn from one another, and introduce people you believe can help each other. Once you get the reputation as an individual who brings people together, people will do the same for you!

TIP #150
Make friends with your neighbors

Look at your town as you would a cocktail party. When you first set up shop, make the rounds, get to know everyone's name, and introduce yourself with a smile. You never know when or how that will pay off.

Case study: Tracy Pamperin, co-founder of The Urban Muse day spa in Denville, New Jersey, went door-to-door to introduce herself to the neighboring businesses when she first moved her spa to town. As though she were chatting at a cocktail party, she asked each person about themselves and their businesses. She worked her way through her community until she'd contacted just about every business owner she could, really getting to know the individuals and what they cared about.

This came in handy very soon after opening her doors. Tracy realized that the town's one-hour parking limit on Main Street posed a real detriment to her business, since her spa treatments generally took longer than an hour. Thanks to the relationships she had built with her neighbors, she was able to enlist their help in an effort to change this policy. Two of the more senior local business owners introduced Tracy to the town administrators, which was key to eventually getting the parking limits extended.

Scan to see a video

TIP #151
Meet people face-to-face

Never underestimate the value of meeting someone face-to-face—or at least voice-to-voice. My father, Max Ramberg, CEO of Hummingbird Group, Inc., who has run three successful companies, has told me this more times than I can count. And he is right.

While we think dashing off a short e-mail or leaving a quick voice message is saving us time, it may actually be wasting our time because of all the back-and-forth caused by one-way communications.

E-mail, texting, voice messages, and Facebook all have their place, but Max says when we communicate electronically, we miss voice inflections and can easily misinterpret the intent of the words. The phone solves that problem. However, when people are on the phone, they're often multitasking and might be distracted by responding to e-mails, surfing the Web, or doing something else at the same time.

Major matters should preferably be handled face-to-face. This allows for a real interactive discussion and deeper understanding of the issues.

How I use this: I recently had an issue with a partner of ours who I thought was not living up to our agreement. We e-mailed back and forth and had a few phone calls, but it just seemed like things were getting worse, not better.

So while I was on vacation in Los Angeles (where his company is based), I called him and asked if we could get a quick coffee. We did. Having the chance to have some old-school face-to-face time solved everything. We talked about my vacation, his new daughter, our favorite architecture, and then, ultimately, business. Suddenly we became two people again rather than two companies. As people, we were able to quickly resolve all our issues.

TIP #152
Creatively contact companies you want to work with

As a small business, it can be very helpful to set up partner-ships with big companies, but getting their attention is much easier said than done.

Nancy Lublin, CEO of the nonprofit DoSomething.org in New York, came up with a solution when her calls to a potential partner were not being returned and her e-mails were going into cyber-wasteland. Instead of requesting a meeting, she sent over a sassy challenge to play them in kick-ball. That's right—a game of kickball! And her challenge was accepted.

As a result, she was able to get eleven of her employees out interacting with eleven employees of the prospective partner company. Those casual relationships eventually paved the way for a substantial business deal.

If you think you might try this, Nancy has one more piece of advice. Don't issue your challenge directly to the top, since it may be hard to get a busy CEO excited about a sports day. You're better off reaching out to the younger, entry-level types, such as an assistant account executive. They are more likely to get excited about the challenge and they'll be the ones to recruit a team.

TIP #153
Meet new people every week

Someone once told me that nothing ever happens if you never leave your house. The same goes for your business. Ari Wallach, founder of Synthesis Corp. in New York, is one of the most networked people I know. He told me that each week he schedules two or three coffees with people he's never met before. Usually he connects with these people through friends or colleagues, but when the well runs dry, he'll cold-invite someone from LinkedIn who has mutual connections. Looking back, he says these meetings have led to 25 percent of his business.

Andrea Sittig-Rolf, a small business advisor and founder of BlitzMasters in Redmond, Washington, has another take. She calls it the "one-hour or two-contacts rule." She says you should allot one hour a day to making calls and developing new leads. If you manage to schedule two new leads in the first ten minutes of calling, quit and move on to other things. If, on the other hand, you spend an hour and wind up with nothing to show for it, you should also quit for the day.

Bottom line: A business that doesn't keep searching for new leads ends up quickly stagnating. You have to keep moving the company forward!

TIP #154
Follow up after you meet someone

Networking is one of the easiest and most effective ways for small business owners to generate leads, but it will end up being totally ineffective if you don't do the follow-up. Everyone blocks time on his or her calendar to attend industry events, whether it be a trade show, conference call, or cocktail hour. But rarely do they schedule time to do a follow-up. Sales and networking expert Alice Heiman in Reno, Nevada, recommends five ways to master the art of successfully following up.

1. **Preplan your follow-up.** Think about why you are going to the event, the types of people you will meet, and what you hope to accomplish. Use that information to start planning your follow-up. Draft an e-mail that you can tailor after the event, or prepare a postcard with a specific message. Or craft a message that you will cut and paste into a LinkedIn or Facebook e-mail. Think about writing an article that pertains to the event so you can post it on your blog and then e-mail that link out after the event.

2. **Use your smartphone.** This works really well at a conference. As you collect cards throughout the day, use Facebook and Twitter to connect with people. Alice also uses CardMunch, a free app that allows you to take a photo of the business card with your smartphone and have it turned into a contact that you can then add to your database.

3. **Schedule time to do the follow-up.** Block at least two opportunities for follow-ups no more than one to three

days following the event. That way if something comes up and usurps the first scheduled time slot, you have another one already planned.

4. **Write notes throughout the day about the people you've met.** This should include information about where you met them, what you talked about, and ways you can work with them. When you get back to your office, put all these notes into your database.

5. **Make plans to see new contacts later.** If you want to develop a relationship that will lead to business, you have to make a connection. Just meeting at the event is not enough. Reach out after the event and get together for coffee or lunch or visit the person's business and take a tour.

TIP #155
Find new leads in your old contacts

If you have a bunch of old business cards you've collected from people over the years lying around gathering dust, pull them out and use them to grow your business. Even if 25 percent of them are old and out of date, 75 percent are likely to still be viable leads.

Una Cote, owner of the business uc, THE SOURCE, in Bridgewater, New Jersey, says she started her meeting and event planning business twenty years ago based on the business contacts she had made as the director of sales and marketing at a large hotel and during her prior jobs in the hospitality industry. When she decided to strike out on her own and try her hand at corporate-event planning, she pulled out every single business card she had collected over the years and laid them out on her dining room table.

She then sent a pitch letter to all of her old contacts saying, "If I ever did anything that you were pleased with and you liked my work ethic and performance, please give me the opportunity to work for you directly in the future." Her appeal worked, and some of those contacts are now her oldest and most valued clients.

TIP #156
Tap your network to stay on top of trends

Twice a year invite ten key people you know in differing businesses to join you in person or on a conference call to chat about what new attitudes, trends, best practices, and challenges they're seeing or experiencing in their world.

Deborah Shane, founder of DeborahShaneToolBox.com in Miami, says that in order to prepare for this meeting, you should develop a list of very specific questions that will yield the precise information you want. For example, "What social-media platforms have helped your company the most and why?" or "What customer-service approach has given you the best retention recently?"

Tip: This is a great way to harvest relevant information and stay on top of key trends and technology. Even if you don't have time to do this every six months, it's worth doing at least once a year.

TIP #157
*Leave the perfect voice mail message—incoming
and outgoing*

How many times have you just deleted a voice mail message because you couldn't understand someone or because the person rambled on for so long that you simply lost interest? Well, you certainly don't want to be the one leaving a message that will get deleted before it's heard or that will annoy the person you're trying to reach.

Steve Hughes, president of Hit Your Stride in Saint Louis, gives some simple and effective tips on leaving the perfect voice-mail message:

• Always leave your phone number at the beginning of the message. People don't want to have to wade through your whole message to get your contact information. Then leave your phone number again at the end of the message.

• Give the other person a suggestion of a good time to call you back if you're going to be busy much of the day— this will reduce potential phone tag.

• Let them know the best way to reach you: work number, cell, e-mail, text, etc.

• Be sure to slow down when you leave your phone number. For some reason, many people tend to speed up when reciting their number, making it very hard to hear and write down. The same goes for leaving e-mail addresses.

When it comes to recording your outgoing message, Steve says you should stand up and release the pressure on your lungs so that you speak with more resonance and with a smile. This will make your message sound nicer and more welcoming than if you record it sitting down. After all, you want the callers to remember how much they like you when they hang up the phone.

By the way, if you don't usually check your voice mail, be sure to let callers know that on your outgoing message. You can even suggest a better way to reach you, such as an e-mail address. I recently called my friend Jen, whose message said, "I don't check voice mail often, so please e-mail me at..." and she left her e-mail address. As someone who hates checking her voice messages, I thought this was just brilliant and I changed my own message the next day!

TIP #158
Write the perfect cold e-mail

Nobody likes to get a novel-length e-mail from someone they don't know. And most people's inboxes are so full that it's likely they may not even read something from a stranger. So when you're sending someone a cold e-mail, Guy Kawasaki, founder of Alltop.com and author of ten best-selling books including *Enchantment*, says you should adhere to these four key rules:

1. **Focus on the subject line.** Make sure your e-mail will not be confused with spam. If you have a friend or contact in common who has referred you, always put that in the subject line instead of just the body of the e-mail. For example, you could make the subject: "Referred by John Smith" or "Friend of John Smith." That will significantly increase the chances that your e-mail at least gets opened.
2. **Keep the e-mail short.** It should be five or six sentences. Think haiku—not *War and Peace*.
3. **Do not attach any files.** If you have something to include, request permission to send it in a second e-mail, or embed it as a link in the body of the e-mail.
4. **Ask for something easy, concrete, and quick.** This gives someone a reason to e-mail you back.

TIP #159
Attend conferences for free

Problem: You want to attend a conference where you'll be able to make valuable contacts or gain industry insight, but you can't afford the ticket.

Solution: Go for free! Dee Marshall, from Raise The Bar in New Jersey, offers up three ways to get your registration fee waived or paid for by someone else:

• Volunteer to work for the conference organizer in exchange for waived registration.

• Contact vendors and exhibitors and inquire about working for them in exchange for a ticket.

• Ask a sponsoring company if they're willing to sponsor you in exchange for some help from you at the conference. Most sponsoring corporations are allowed a number of registrations and typically don't use them all.

Watch out! If you are going to offer to work for someone, you *have* to do the work. Make sure the job they're asking you to do leaves you with enough time during the conference to make the contacts you need!

TIP #160
Turn your inexperience into an asset

Successful people often enjoy helping those who are just starting out. Even though you may feel a little uncomfortable asking for advice or assistance, don't let that stop you.

Case study: Arien Rozelle, a young entrepreneur from New York City who runs FeelingAnxious PR, truly believes, "When in doubt, ask. The worst thing they can say is no."

As a burgeoning entrepreneur, this attitude has helped Arien immensely. From tech problems to business opportunities to looking for an intern, asking has been the ticket.

Arien is great with media and generating publicity, but not quite the best with accounting and finance. When she needed help with accounting, she decided to tap her network of friends (and friends of friends). She did the same when she needed a new logo, help with her IT, and setting up her LLC. A number of people were happy to help. Eventually she was able to pay for the work, and now she refers other paying clients. Just bear in mind that asking someone to work for free isn't easy.

Her technique for asking is simple:

1. Ask for things in a friendly, understanding, and well-informed way. It's not about being fake or pushy.

2. Be sensitive about the nature of the relationship. Take cues from people's responses. If it doesn't look like they want to help, take the hint and back off.

3. And of course, be truly thankful. Send a thank-you note or gift and remember to return the favor down the road.

CHAPTER TEN

CONTROLLING COSTS

How to keep expenses in check

TIP #161   Think like a start-up   236

TIP #162   How to get relief from your credit card
           company   237

TIP #163   Don't itemize expenses   238

TIP #164   Negotiate deals for prepaying
           your suppliers   239

TIP #165   Negotiate flat rates for legal and
           accounting fees   240

TIP #166   Be honest when you can't pay   241

TIP #167   Join a co-op for bulk-rate pricing   242

TIP #168   Make sure you're invoicing
           clients correctly   244

TIP #169   Negotiate reasonable rent   245

TIP #170   Start with small-quantity orders from
           your manufacturers   246

TIP #171   Avoid signing personal guarantees   247

TIP #161
Think like a start-up

Having cash on hand, solid contacts in your industry, and success is great, but it can also lead to laziness and stifle creativity. Why? Because when you don't have much, you are forced to be creative and energetic to get things done. Once you have the money and connections, it's easy to rely on them, but in the process you may end up spending wastefully.

Scott Gerber, founder of the Young Entrepreneur Council in New York City, says there's an easy way to get around this. Before going forward with any large decision, ask yourself and your team, "If we didn't have the money to pay for this, how would we reach the same goal?" This simple question will prompt everyone to see if there is a more efficient way to do things.

TIP #162
How to get relief from your credit card company

When your back is against the wall, your credit card company may not be the first place you'd look for help. However, bankruptcy lawyer Hagop Bedoyan of Fresno, California, says, "You'd be making a big mistake if you don't reach out to the credit card companies directly for some debt relief. The only catch is that you have to approach them the right way if you want it to work."

Hagop says credit card companies are very often willing to reduce amounts owed by borrowers if they receive the request letter from a bankruptcy attorney proposing a discounted settlement. By having the settlement offer go out on a bankruptcy attorney's letterhead, the creditor knows that failure to settle the unpaid debt may result in a bankruptcy filing where they would get nothing. He says he's always amazed at how effective this appeal can be.

If you're not quite ready to hire a bankruptcy lawyer, Hagop suggests contacting a nonprofit debt-consolidation program such as Consumer Credit Counseling Services (CCCS) or Springboard. Unlike the "for-profit" companies that advertise on late-night TV, these organizations, he says, actually can help consumers lower or eliminate their debt. And they do this without charging the consumer exorbitant fees, since they receive funding from grant money in the credit community. He suggests that somebody with debt problems try this approach first before seeing a lawyer, as it may be all they need.

TIP #163
Don't itemize expenses

Itemizing expenses for clients is a time-consuming annoyance! Nicholas Eisenberger, founder of Pure Energy Partners in New York, decided to stop doing it. Instead, he charges his clients a flat monthly fee for expenses.

Of course this fee has to be negotiated up front, but it saves all the hassle later on. Surely nobody on your team wants to gather together Starbucks and hotel and taxi receipts to send to your client. And it's likely nobody on the client's team wants to have to go through all of those receipts. Let your client know that every moment you spend organizing receipts for them is time not spent working on the core of your assignment. Setting a flat fee is simply more efficient!

TIP #164
Negotiate deals for prepaying your suppliers

Rohit Arora, CEO of Biz2Credit in New York City, says always ask your suppliers if they'll give you a discount if you pay in advance. By doing this, you'll save money and also guarantee that you always pay on time.

Case study: Sumit Kumar of Summit Telecom in New York sells prepaid phone cards, and gets between a 2 and 35 percent discount from his card vendors if he pays up front by cash or check. When you're talking about a $500,000-monthly business, this adds up to quite a bit of money!

TIP #165
Negotiate flat rates for legal and accounting fees

Take control of your legal and accounting fees by negotiating a flat rate instead of paying by the hour. This way you can better anticipate your cost and keep your budget in check.

Kenneth Trinder, a former lawyer and CEO of Virginia-based EOS Surfaces, says that while in the past many professionals would frown upon setting a fixed rate, it has become more customary over the last several years. Instead of getting an hourly rate, explain your needs thoroughly and negotiate for an up-front price to perform the work.

Watch out! If you do this, you have to be very clear about what is and what is not included for this fee. You'd hate to get less than you bargained for.

TIP #166
Be honest when you can't pay

Just as you do not like being surprised by receiving a late payment, you don't want to surprise someone else when you can't pay on time.

So be honest. If you know you have a tricky stretch coming where your cash will be negative or tight, call your major vendors and let them know ahead of time. These situations are never easy, but you may find that the vendor will be more flexible about the situation if you initiate the conversation and let them know you intend to work it out.

If you want to preserve the relationship with a particular supplier/vendor, here's one way to go. Offer to start paying COD for any new purchases and pay a little something extra every month to pay off what you owe them.

TIP #167
Join a co-op for bulk-rate pricing

Joining up with other businesses that purchase items, services, and supplies similar to the ones you purchase—everything from bulk packaging to health care plans—is a great way to get large-volume discounts and also receive better service. You may be able to negotiate for higher levels of tech support, quicker access to replacement parts, and better help-desk technicians if you have the clout of a large contract to back you up.

How do you do this?

1. The easiest way is by joining an existing buying cooperative in your business category. Check with your trade associations to find one, and then contact them about joining up. For example, if you were in the concrete products industry you could join the Concrete Products Cooperative. You would pay a fee to become a member, and as a member you would qualify for the same kind of steep supplier discounts enjoyed by big business customers with large-volume contracts.

2. You can form your own buying cooperative with as many or as few members as you wish. However, this is not something to be done casually. You need to set up a legal entity and then negotiate contracts with suppliers. That said, it's quite possible to do and it could mean the difference between survival and failure for an independent business. For more information on the nuts and bolts of doing something like this, contact the National Cooperative Business Association (NCBA).

Case study: Thanexus, Inc., is a funeral-service cooperative offering human resources, marketing, and financial services to New Jersey's independently owned funeral homes. Members enjoy the benefits of a relationship where both Thanexus and the funeral home share employment-related responsibilities. The roughly one hundred members use the cooperative to contractually allocate and share traditional employer responsibilities, such as payroll and taxes, human resources guidance, and employment-law compliance. By working together, they've saved a lot of money.

TIP #168
Make sure you're invoicing clients correctly

Problem: Your corporate clients are paying you late.

Solution: Double-check the paperwork you supplied!

When it comes to the "accounts payable" department at big corporations, the devil often lies in the details.

For example, did you send the invoice to the attention of the correct person? Was the work done or materials supplied correctly identified? Does the company require backup information or a purchase-order number that might have been left out? A small mistake in paperwork can easily derail an invoice and put it into an endless holding pattern. However, a mere ten minutes of double-checking on your end can put your invoice back on track to be paid.

Gene Marks, founder of The Marks Group in Bala Cynwyd, Pennsylvania, says he learned this the hard way. After waiting months to get paid by one of his large clients, he discovered that the delayed invoice didn't have a purchase-order number on it. As a result, it wasn't entered properly into their system and it never got paid.

Gene says that most of the large companies he works with have very formalized processes and procedures that work great until something goes wrong—such as a missing purchase-order number—and then it's hard to get your invoice through the system.

Gene also says that you should make sure you fill out all required forms—such as a W-9—in advance too. Missing forms is another way to derail an on-time payment.

TIP #169
Negotiate reasonable rent

Before you agree to any lease, do some research to understand how willing your landlord might be to negotiate. International venture-capital lawyer Jennifer Hill says to do your homework. Hunt through the local real estate newspapers to see if there's any mention of the landlord or the building you are considering. Pay close attention to any talk or mention about vacancy rates or financial difficulties for this landlord's properties. If the landlord has high vacancies, you might be able to use that as leverage to negotiate a better rate.

Also, check with your city planning office, especially if you are in retail, to find out if there are new projects being planned in your area that could affect your foot traffic. If there's going to be construction near your store in the short term, it may reduce foot traffic and become a real factor in the success of your location. Use this information to negotiate your rent.

In the long term, you want to know what's being built to see if it will benefit your business or harm it. If it's a luxury high-rise, that might be good, but if it's a sewage-treatment center or includes other businesses that may be detrimental to your brand, you might want to think about finding a location somewhere else.

And Jen says, once you're in the building, be sure to become friends with the other tenants. If economic conditions or building conditions change, it will be helpful to go to your landlord as a group. There is strength in numbers!

TIP #170
Start with small-quantity orders from your manufacturers

When you're manufacturing a new product, always order a small amount first (even though it may cost you more initially). Don't cave in to the manufacturer's standard Minimum Order Quantity (MOQ) just to get a price break.

Brent Wagner runs the San Diego sporting-goods brand The Day of Games and has had a lot of experience with manufacturers. He says the MOQs are *always* negotiable and you don't want to end up with a product that is not exactly as you envisioned. When dealing with international manufacturers, the quality control may not be the same as in the States. He notes that even if you have quality-control systems in place, you still might end up with a product that isn't 100 percent perfect. Brent has received bocce sets with the wrong colors, the wrong zippers on the bags, and incorrect packaging. Even after having weekly quality-control calls and reviewing digital photos directly from the factory, small problems with new products still occasionally occur. This can be alleviated by ordering small amounts first, then increasing the orders as you approve the finished and delivered goods.

TIP #171
Avoid signing personal guarantees

If you're asked to sign a personal guarantee—and chances are you will be asked to do so if you get a commercial lease or a line of credit—try *not* to sign it.

Easier said than done, I know. But it's worth a try. Attorney Hagop Bedoyan says a significant number of personal bankruptcy cases he sees are all a result of someone signing a personal guarantee.

So here are some things to try:

• Show that your business itself has sufficient assets or earnings to be responsible for the loan or lease. The hope is that this makes the lender or landlord feel comfortable enough that they'll get the money owed them, so that they won't require the guarantee.

• Try to negotiate that the guarantee covers only up to a certain dollar amount or only kicks in under certain circumstances.

• Write into your loan covenants or lease that once certain goals are achieved, the guarantees will be removed. Some banks and landlords will agree to this, some won't.

What you are trying to do here is limit your exposure, so it makes sense to try everything you can!

CHAPTER ELEVEN

RUNNING THE OFFICE

Keeping things running smoothly

TIP #172   Document your processes   250

TIP #173   Back up your hard drive   251

TIP #174   Start your day with a top-five list   253

TIP #175   Keep yourself organized   254

TIP #176   Manage your time with a task
           time log   255

TIP #177   Calendar everything   257

TIP #178   Clear out your inbox   258

TIP #179   Knock off the easy stuff first   260

TIP #180   Simplify everything   261

TIP #181   Prioritize by allocating your energy
           across projects   262

TIP #182   Plan an office organization day   264

TIP #183   Protect your accounts from scammers   265

TIP #172
Document your processes

We like to call this the "What if someone gets hit by a bus" tip. Basically, do you have the systems in place to continue work if someone can't come in? Do you know where all their work is kept and how it's organized? Most of us don't. But we should.

Case study: Justin Hong is the managing partner of Los Angeles–based Highly Relevant, an Internet marketing firm specializing in search engine optimization (SEO). He says when they first started up, there were only two people on their team who knew how to implement their SEO strategies, and if they didn't execute the projects themselves or tell other people what to do, their entire business came to a standstill.

In 2011, Justin and his team decided to lay out every single step in their SEO process, documenting every detail in both text and video. Suddenly, members of the team who were not as well versed in putting together these campaigns could go through step-by-step and execute one. In other words, they didn't need to wait for those two people.

In addition, they found an unexpected benefit to creating these documents. Looking at the process closely allowed the team to identify certain steps that could be either outsourced or executed by people other than their core team. This allowed them to free up their own time to work on more high-value tasks, such as meeting with prospects, developing business relationships, and setting goals.

TIP #173
Back up your hard drive

If you have ever had your computer crash, you know how disruptive it is. It happened to me a few years ago and I'm still kicking myself that I didn't have my hard drive backed up.

So listen to me. Back up your files in the cloud. Right now! Really. Immediately close this book and do it if you have not done it already. This is assuming you still use your hard drive—some of you may already do all of your work in the cloud.

If all this does not mean anything to you—we are simply saying sign up for a Web-based service that backs up your information for you. There are plenty of solutions out there—both free and paid. Even the most basic services make it easy—they just back up everything you have on your hard drive for you. You don't have to do a thing once you sign up!

Dan Ackerman, a technology editor at CNET, says that he backs up all of his important information in three places—his hard drive, an external hard drive, and the cloud. After my computer crashed, I now do the same.

Tip: Laura Yecies of SugarSync, a San Francisco–based online backup service, says the cloud offers more than just backup. For small business owners, the benefits include: accessing the files anywhere and never losing something when moving from one computer or device to another (very valuable for those of us who are juggling multiple devices from laptops to smartphones and tablets). Working in the cloud also enables you to send, share, and seamlessly collaborate with customers, colleagues, and employees. And one of the best features is the fact that it can simplify the awkwardness of working between different operating systems.

Added tip: If you have not yet set up your backup system or you're not positive it's working *and* if you have a really important document, send it to yourself via a Gmail, Hotmail, or Yahoo account or something similar. That way it's saved somewhere besides your computer.

TIP #174
Start your day with a top-five list

The moment you walk into your office (or before you leave the day before), write down the top five things you need to get done that day listed in order of importance. Cameron Herold, founder of BackPocket COO in Vancouver, Canada, says he does this every day and then starts with item number one and works his way down the list. He encourages everyone on his team to get through at least number three on the list before they look at their e-mail inbox.

How I use this: I'm a big fan of lists. Particularly because I love the thrill of crossing something off! That said, I can also become completely engrossed in busywork and can easily be swayed by it to procrastinate. Writing down my priorities for the day really helps me focus—I already know what I need to get done, but having it actually in front of me on a piece of paper somehow motivates me to do it.

Tip: Nell Merlino, CEO of New York–based Make Mine a Million $ Business, says that every morning she writes a to-do list for herself. She then highlights the tasks that only she can do herself. The rest she delegates out to her staff.

TIP #175
Keep yourself organized

Problem: Half of your files are digital and the other half are hard copies and you can never find what you need when you need it.

Solution: Cara Natterson, owner of Worry Proof MD (and one of the most organized people I know), says she has three suggestions that help keep her business neat, clean, and well organized:

1. Create digital files with the same name as your physical files so you keep relevant documents in groups.

2. Keep a supply of empty file jackets, blank labels, and a label maker. File things immediately. If you don't have the supplies, chances are important documents will end up in a big pile.

3. If you have meetings that necessitate that you record information afterward, schedule an extra ten minutes in your calendar. When the meeting is finished, take that extra time to do the documentation. Make that part of your process.

TIP #176
Manage your time with a task time log

Let's face it, one of the most common complaints we hear from entrepreneurs is, "I don't have time…"

So how *do* you find time?

Paul Karofsky, founder and CEO of Palm Beach Gardens, Florida–based Transition Consulting Group, says, "It's not about time but about priority. When we say we don't have enough time to perform a certain task, what we're really saying is that other tasks took precedence or were more enjoyable to do."

Paul says there's an old tool called a "task time log," which is often poorly understood, but can literally free up your schedule. It's a simple log sheet that breaks down the day into fifteen-minute intervals. Take a week or so and fill out the log with the tasks you performed and how much satisfaction you got out of completing them (personal and professional). This will clearly spell out for you how you spend your time, and it'll likely be eye-opening.

You can then look for the least-enjoyable and least-important tasks to see how many of those can be delegated. You can use the chart below:

Time	Task Performed	Importance (High, Med, Low)	Are you good at this task (yes, somewhat, no)	How enjoyable (very, somewhat, not)
7:00 AM				
7:15 AM				
7:30 AM				
7:45 AM				
6:00 PM				

(Continued)

Time	Task Performed	Importance (High, Med, Low)	Are you good at this task (yes, somewhat, no)	How enjoyable (very, somewhat, not)
6:15 PM				
6:30 PM				
6:45 PM				
7:00 PM				

TIP #177
Calendar everything

Put every single thing you need to do—large or small—into your digital calendar. Dhenu Savla, an immigration attorney and founder of SwagatUSA in Chicago, says that the more you get into the habit of calendaring things, the better you can manage the multiple roles you are no doubt playing as a small business owner.

It's easy to get caught up with what we're doing at any given time, and it's hard to remember things such as following up with a lead, scheduling the exterminator for the office, or interviewing a new candidate when you're in the thick of doing something else. Dhenu says that client development, business-marketing meetings, as well as family events need to be written down or they'll likely get forgotten in the busy ups-and-downs of the day.

How I use this: You would all laugh to see how crazy my calendar is! It seamlessly combines my MSNBC interviews, GoodSearch business, and life. The only hope for me to remember all of these competing interests is through my calendar. And, I'm embarrassed to say, my husband and I often communicate via our calendars. So every time I set something up that affects his schedule (e.g., if I have to be at a meeting early, he'll have to take the kids to school, or we have a dinner to attend together), I simply send him a calendar appointment so that it's placed on his schedule as well.

TIP #178
Clear out your inbox

Professional organizers will tell you that when it comes to keeping your closet chaos-free, if you haven't worn a particular piece of clothing in a year, throw it out. Rod Kurtz, executive editor of the *Huffington Post* "Small Business" section, says he thinks of his e-mail inbox the same way. Except that every item in his inbox has an expiration date of just one day.

Like most professionals in the digital age, Rod's inbox is his nerve center, or as he calls it, his "mission control." It's filled with conversations about things he needs to do, meetings to attend, and of course, there's just a bunch of junk. In less than two years in his current job, he's received more than fifty thousand e-mails.

So he came up with a basic ground rule: If he hasn't read, responded to, or acted on an e-mail within one day, it simply gets deleted. It may sound like an impossible goal, but Rod ends every day with his inbox at zero, or gets as close as he can.

So how does he do this?

• He immediately marks as "read" anything that is not relevant.

• Throughout the day, he fires off quick responses to any new e-mails that come in.

• He spends the last fifteen minutes of each day dealing with any unanswered e-mails.

• Anything he needs to save, he catalogs in a folder.

• For things he needs to act upon but doesn't have the time to do at that particular moment, he keeps it marked as "unread" so it stands out like a to-do list. If he cannot deal with it that day, he forwards a copy of it to himself so it appears fresh the next day.

Rod says he does not block off a period of "e-mail time" per se, but he does try to get to his e-mail in batches.

How I use this: I admit, this is a hard one and I'm not great at it. But last year I vowed to start off the New Year with less than a page of e-mails in my inbox, and it truly felt like an enormous weight had been taken off my shoulders when I did it! The key, of course, is to keep the momentum going.

Suggestion: If you're working on something that takes your full concentration, turn off the e-mail alert that pops up on your computer screen every time you get your e-mail. That annoying little distraction will cause you to lose time.

TIP #179
Knock off the easy stuff first

When scheduling projects, consider how long something will take, and where it stands in the pecking order of things to do.

When you are considering which things to start first, see if you can knock some things out fast, even if they are less important. It's a good idea to take care of those items before assigning your team a long project that will take up a lot of resources.

How I use this: When we decide on priorities at GoodSearch, we always attach a time estimate to them. If something is incredibly important but will take a month to complete, we try to knock off some quicker projects first, even if they're less critical.

One way you can figure out your priorities is to put all your projects into a matrix—with the top being "Lengthy" and "Quick" (referring to how much time each will take) and the side being "Critical" and "Not critical." Clearly the critical projects that won't take up much time should go ahead of the rest. After that, you can use your judgment based on this map as a guide to how to schedule everything else.

Duration

		Lengthy	Quick
Importance	Critical		
	Not critical		

TIP #180
Simplify everything

Complexity is the enemy of every small business. Oftentimes, we make things much more complex than they need to be. Once a process is in place and working, it may be hard to simplify it, but if you can, it makes an enormous difference in terms of efficiency, effectiveness, and ultimately the bottom line. Kevin Ou, founder of Lumenere and KEV!NOU // PHOTOGRAPHY in Los Angeles, suggests the following ideas for jumpstarting your simplification process:

• Ask "why do we do...(list the task or process)?" Simply asking the question will likely point out some areas that could be improved upon. In fact, there are usually elements that your employees already quietly complain about but haven't shared with the group yet. Now's the time.

• Ask your employees to submit one specific suggestion for something that needs to be simplified. People who are in the trenches are the ones who have firsthand knowledge about which tasks need streamlining.

Make sure your employees can give suggestions without any repercussions (even hurt feelings). If someone on your team believes a process is getting too complex, they need to feel free to speak to their manager or you about it honestly.

TIP #181
Prioritize by allocating your energy across projects

Problem: You and your team are excited about multiple projects that all seem to be on the "high priority" list—but you don't have enough time or resources to get them all done.

Solution: Prioritize your projects based on where your time and energy should be allocated on a daily basis. Scott Belsky, founder of the Behance Network and author of *Making Ideas Happen*, says to gather your team together around a whiteboard and write the names of all their major projects on small cards. On the whiteboard, draw a line, and on one end write "Extreme"; on the other, write "Idle." This represents the spectrum of energy that should be spent on each project.

Extreme  **Idle**

Next, your team should place the cards along the line according to their importance and how much collective focus each project should get from the team. At first, you'll probably find that too many projects are being placed near the "Extreme" end of the spectrum. This is a natural tendency, because each member of your team who is spearheading a specific project will likely think that their project is of top importance. However, this exercise will serve as a jumping-off point for you and your team to evaluate each project and then re-place it on the line in order to come up with a true list of priorities. By the way, be prepared for disagreements along the way. They're inevitable, but are of great value because they help you collectively prioritize.

Remember, these are tough decisions to make, and as the boss, if the debate does not get to a clear resolution, ultimately you will have to decide the direction you want your company to go. Be strict about this. It does not help anyone if you end up with too many things marked "Extreme" and then they don't get done because you have limited resources.

Tip: Once you figure out your priorities, go to tip #179 to help you schedule them.

TIP #182
Plan an office organization day

Once a year, create an organization day in your office. Julie Morgenstern, a professional organizer and author of *Organizing from the Inside Out*, says this will force your entire team to clean up their workstations, their computer files, and the office. Reducing this clutter makes things run more smoothly for everyone.

Here is how you prepare for the day:

• Assign a leader. This is the person who is going to get everyone excited and enthused about the cleanup and make sure it happens.

• Order supplies in advance, such as garbage bags and storage boxes, so that everything you need is on hand when the big day comes.

• Also prepare by creating a "keep" and "toss" guideline for shared items in the office.

Decide ahead of time if you need to create new locations for things or special storage areas so that you don't end up creating a pile of stuff that doesn't have a home. The last thing you want is to create a new pile that doesn't get addressed until the next organization day.

TIP #183
Protect your accounts from scammers

Once a year, have a discussion with your employees about social engineering. And if you don't know what that means, all the more reason to have that discussion!

Social engineering is basically a criminal's (or at least a clever trickster's) way of getting you to give over private information that will allow them to steal from, or spy on, your online accounts. If you have received any e-mails from a stranger asking for your bank account information to transfer money out of their country, then you've already been a target!!

While most of us think that we're too smart to fall for these online confidence games, you'd be surprised. Dan Ackerman, a senior editor at CNET, says that every once in a while even he catches himself almost clicking on a dicey link. While we all know not to answer the e-mail from that stranger, many of us might have been tempted to click on the link asking us if we want to see who's looked at our Facebook profile recently.

Be forewarned that your staff may not be keen on following the advice below, since it can mean a lot of extra steps on their part. For this reason, it's important to let them know the consequences for the business if thieves gain access to the company's accounts. They surely don't want to be the person responsible for any security breach into your company's database or records.

Here are a couple of rules of thumb to share with your employees:

• If you get an e-mail from an institution you work with, such as your bank, PayPal, or eBay, and it's asking you to click on something to read a message or update information, *don't click through.* Ignore the link, go directly to the company's website from your web browser, and log in from there to take care of any business.

• Beware of links and shared content on social networks such as Facebook that seem out of character for your friends. You may click on an interesting-looking video and then get a request from an app or video player to grant some kind of Facebook permission. That's a red flag, unless it's a Facebook app you know already, such as FarmVille or Spotify. Otherwise, you could be giving a third party access to both your Facebook account and the Facebook product and company pages you administer.

• The best way to spot a fake "phishing" e-mail is by simply staying alert. If you are observant, fake e-mails are often obvious because of graphics that are a little off and text that's riddled with awkward phrasing and punctuation errors.

Use multiple passwords: Dan also says to be sure to use different passwords for every site. The easiest way for scammers to gain access to your accounts is to find the username and password for one of them, because so many of us use the same password for all of our accounts. While it's hard to remember a bunch of different passwords, it's worth it. Come up with a system that works for you to create password variations for different sites—but keep the methodology to yourself!

Important: Also be sure to change your internal passwords when an employee leaves your company, whether it was their own doing or they were fired. While this may seem paranoid, especially if they left on good terms, you do not want people who are no longer working for you to have access to your company's information.

Thanks so much for taking the time to read this book. If you used any of these tips in your business, we'd love to hear how it worked out. If you have any of your own tips you'd like to share, we'd love to hear those too. Please join the conversation at www.itsyourbusinessbook.com.

ABOUT THE AUTHORS

JJ Ramberg

JJ is the host of MSNBC's *Your Business*, the only television show dedicated to issues affecting small business owners. Now in its sixth season, the program has profiled thousands of entrepreneurs and has offered advice from countless experts and investors.

In 2005, JJ and her brother, Ken, founded GoodSearch .com, a company that turns your everyday activities into ways to give back to your favorite cause. GoodSearch has raised around $10 million for its participating charities and schools.

JJ has bounced between entrepreneurial activities and journalism throughout her career, having worked as a producer, reporter, and host for CNN and CNNfn, a producer on *Dateline NBC*, and the director of business development at Cooking.com.

JJ holds her MBA from the Stanford University Graduate School of Business and her bachelor of arts from Duke University. She lives in Brooklyn, New York, with her husband and three children.

Lisa Everson

Lisa joined MSNBC in 2006 to help launch *Your Business*, producing dozens of stories for the program and masterminding the show's broadcast from some of the biggest events in small business, including the Inc. 500 Conference, the *New York Times* Small Business Summit, and the Consumer Electronics Show.

Lisa also spent seven years at ABC News producing programs for cable TV outlets including A&E, American Movie Classics, Discovery, History channel, and truTV. For A&E, Lisa produced biographies on business figures such as Thomas Watson Jr., legendary CEO of IBM, and The Home Depot founders Arthur Blank and Bernie Marcus; political figures such as Muammar Gaddafi and Laura Bush; and actors, including Julia Louis-Dreyfus and Robin Williams. For Discovery, she scaled the tallest building in the world for *7 Wonders of Engineering*, and uncovered new evidence in the legendary Boston Strangler case. For the History channel, Lisa worked with Cokie Roberts telling the story of our Founding Mothers.

Lisa started her career working with the award-winning filmmakers Gene Feldman and Suzette Winter, with whom she worked on numerous documentaries about Hollywood legends such as Gary Cooper, Ingrid Bergman, and Jack Lemmon. These films are now part of the Feldman Collection housed at the George Eastman House International Museum of Photography and Film in Rochester, New York.

Lisa has a bachelor of arts in History and Political Science from Stony Brook University. She lives in Park Ridge, New Jersey, with her husband and two children.

Frank Silverstein

Frank is a television newsmagazine reporter. He came to MSNBC in 2006 as part of the start-up team on *Your Business*.

He spent the bulk of his career at ABC News, where he was assigned to *20/20*, *Primetime Live*, and *DayOne*. He developed stories and produced reports for Robert Krulwich, John Hockenberry, Bob Brown, John Stossel, Barbara Walters, Diane Sawyer, and others. He has also worked at CBS, CNN, and CNBC producing stories and investigative reports on the economy, politics, corruption, religion, medicine, and the military.

Frank has also produced several independent documentaries, was an animator on CBS's *Pee-wee's Playhouse*, and began his career working for filmmaker William Greaves.

Frank holds a master's degree in American History from Columbia and a bachelor of arts degree from Yale. He lives in Hastings-on-Hudson, New York, with his wife and daughter.

ACKNOWLEDGMENTS

Writing this book was a team effort. The three of us want to thank first and foremost the thousands of entrepreneurs, investors, and experts we have met over the past six years who have graciously given so much of their time to share their experiences with us. In particular, we'd like to give special acknowledgment to the more than two hundred people we re-interviewed in order to really hone in on their best pieces of advice for this book.

Here at MSNBC there is a single individual to whom we owe an incalculable debt. Scott Leon, the executive producer of *Your Business*, has guided us and our network into the world of small business reporting. As the creator of this show, you truly filled a need for small business owners. The direction and guidance you have given us as TV producers has carried over into the writing of the book—including the larger vision of making sure we always find and provide a valuable "lesson" in each and every one of our segments. That key ingredient has echoed in our heads again and again as we sat down to write this book. Your creativity ensures that we continue to look at our world in new ways, and we've learned a tremendous amount from you. We are very proud to be part of your team and can't thank you enough for your leadership.

Dawn Stackhouse, David Foster, Jessica Shim, Andrew Littell, and Christine Cataldi, as part of the *Your Business* team, you are really part of this book as well. We thank you for your expertise and point of view, which are incorporated in these pages.

Lou Paskalis and the entire team at American Express, your commitment to small business has inspired us and allowed us to do our job. Thank you for all your support.

Bonnie Solow, our agent—how lucky we are to have met you. Thank you for guiding three television people through the world of publishing. And Rick Wolff, our editor, we appreciate every single meeting we had with you as you helped shape this idea into a book.

A special thanks to MSNBC president Phil Griffin for giving us the green light to work on this project and to Stu Goldstein for helping us dot the i's and cross the t's so we could get to the finish line.

JJ Ramberg

I would like to give a special thanks to my father and mother, Max and Connie Ramberg, who were the original entrepreneurs in my life. It's simply by their example as people and as business owners that I try to always lead my life. To my husband, Scott Glass, thanks for being my nightly focus group and for all of those days you took on everything at home so that I could be out writing. I surely would not have finished this book if you were not so fabulous. Calder, Connor, and Clover: Although you're too little to read this now, I hope that one day this book helps you as you go off into the world to start your own ventures or join others. My siblings Brad Ramberg and Joanna Moore, Ken and Bari Ramberg, and Tom and Melanie Staggs, thank you for always being there for me. I couldn't ask for a better group of big brothers and sisters. Ken, I am incredibly lucky to have you as my business partner. I have learned more from you about running a company in the past six years than I could ever have imagined. Scott Garell, thanks for arriving when you did!

Finally, Lisa and Frank, thank you for having the patience to deal with someone who does not have the time to say the second J. The show and this book would not be the same without your curiosity, creativity, and insight.

Lisa Everson

To all of the very special men in my life, you have surrounded me with love and support for as long as I can remember. To my father, Jack Everson, thank you for being my most steadfast supporter and encouraging me to shoot for the moon. To my brother, John Everson, who has been the best sounding board and middle-of-the-night counselor a sister could ask for. To my husband, Glen Schauer, for picking up the slack and taking care of all the business of our crazy lives when I was too busy to do anything but work on this project. You are my rock; nothing would be possible without you by my side. And to my little boy, Oliver, who lights up the room and cheers my spirit on a daily basis. I hope when you are older and can read this, you'll understand why Mommy was at the computer and not able to play trains as much as you would have liked.

To my mother, Elizabeth Ann Everson, though memories fade, your zeal for life and spirit is not forgotten.

To my coauthors: JJ, you have taught me more than you'll ever know about small business, time efficiency, and confidence. It's been a distinct pleasure to work with you on the show and on this book. Frank, our walks for morning coffee wouldn't be the same without your stimulating conversation. If I remember correctly, the idea for writing a book started on one of those walks. I'm so glad it did and I look forward to what other ideas hatch on future coffee runs.

Frank Silverstein

I would like to thank JJ and Lisa, who are both so smart and fun that I genuinely cherish all those hours we spent locked in airless conference rooms working together on this book. And I would also like to thank George Stoney, whose generous advice and guidance launched my career.

My greatest gratitude is to my parents, Marilyn Cooper Silverstein and Josef Silverstein. I am proud to have been infected with their adventurous spirit and boundless curiosity. My brother, Gordon Silverstein, is also owed enormous thanks for his many hours of late-night advice. I must thank my daughter, Maya, for her fearless spirit of independence. She is a constant challenge to any complacency and I love her for it, and I like to think that something of her energy animates this book as well. Above all, however, my deepest debt is to my wife, Esther Brumberg, who has given me her love and trust and an archivist's determination to find the tiny strands of order in the chaos of our lives, which makes everything possible.

CONTRIBUTOR INDEX

Ackerman, Dan 251
Armstrong, Deb 191
Arnof-Fenn, Paige 158
Aronovich, Ian 35
Arora, Rohit 239
Bagley, Michael 123
Bargh, John 128
Barry, Brett 120
Bedoyan, Hagop 237
Belsky, Scott 262
Bentley, Gayla 17
Berkus, David 45
Berliner, Andy 59
Berliner, Rachel 59
Bird, Sterrin 164
Bitterman, Mark 202
Blank, Arthur 135
Blasevick, Denise 71
Blasingame, Jim 62
Bosma, Michael 89
Bostock, Matt 165
Boyer, Shari 200
Brodsky, Norm 154
Brookhart, Josh xi
Budde, Erik 56
Carlson, Mari-
   anne 25

Carney, Dana 63
Chaiken, Julie 108
Chan, Hamilton 178
Chao, John 194
Chartrand, Tanya 128
Cialdini, Robert 160
Clemmons, Mike 157
Cohen, Dan 138
Cohen, Ivy 30
Coles, Sharon 97
Corcoran,
   Barbara 17
Corp, Katherine xii
Corp, Kimberly 159
Cote, Una 228
Cuddy, Amy 63
Curleigh, James 114
Dalton, Craig 205
Daskal, Lolly 98
Dean, Will 46
DeBaise, Colleen 216
DeFilippis, Tony 16
Dering, Peter 84
Dethloff, Clay 37
DiGiambattista,
   Belinda 80
Dontcheva, Silvia 26

Duke, Linda 206
Edmond, Alfred
   Jr. 70
Egelhoff, Tom 210
Eisenberger,
   Nicholas 238
Emerson, Melinda 220
Engels, Kristy 119
Erickson, Gary 27
Eshman, Mark 181
Everson, Lisa xii
Farrah, Pat 135
Fulton, Jenny 150
Gaines, Camille 82
Galbraith, Laura 129
Garell, Scott xiii
Gelburd,
   Lawrence 183
Gerber, Scott 236
Gignilliat, Bibby 82
Givens, Menina 128
Glass, Scott 76
Godsoe, Eden 168
Goldberg, Dave 176
Goldberg, Jason 6
Good, John 9
Gould, Gordon 168

Griffith, Scott 66
Grizont, Stella 172
Haber, Neal 92
Halligan, Brian 2
Harris, Ashleigh 204
Haywood, Leslie 77
Hecht, Brian 34
Heiman, Alice 226
Hermelin, Julie 50
Herold, Cameron 253
Hess, Judi 54
Hill, Jennifer 245
Hinkle, Brandon 86
Hoagland-Smith,
   Leanne 130
Hong, Justin 250
Hughens, Dana 88
Hughes, Steve 230
Huntington, John 175
Huntington,
   Melissa 175
Intelisano, Ross 79
Jandula, Thomas 175
John, Daymond 17
Joy, James 171
Kaplan, Rob 67
Karofsky, Paul 255
Katkar, Rama 85
Kaufman, Eric 216
Kaufman, Jack E. 162
Kaufman, Nina 51
Kawasaki, Guy 232
Kim, Angela Jia 213

Koch, Jim 69
Kumar, Sumit 239
Kurcz, Kara 196
Kurtz, Rod 199
Kushnir, Julia 123
Lazar, David 108
Lazzari, Lani 77
Lesonsky, Rieva 145
Levin, Robert 124
L'Heureux, A. K. 129
Light, Paulette 50
Lightfoot, Karla 174
Livingstone,
   Robert 182
Lopez, Heather 192
Lopez, Lindsay 212
Lublin, Nancy 224
Lynch, Bill 138
Lyne, Susan 99
Majcher, Marley 187
Marcus, Bernie 135
Marks, Gene 244
Marshall, Dee 233
Martin, Dan 39
Martin, Steve 203
McCann, Jim 59
McKeown, Les 186
Meeks, Rodney 97
Mehta, Monica 15
Merlino, Nell 253
Michalowicz,
   Mike 153
Miller, Charlena 201

Miller, Terry 126
Moltz, Barry 75
Moman, Matt 157
Morgan, Howard 5
Morgenstern,
   Julie 264
Mycoskie, Blake 81
Nagle, Thomas 122
Natan, Eli 121
Natterson, Cara 254
Navon, Gadi 31
Nemo, Ben 214
Neptune, Jean-
   Luc 125
Nichols, Courtney 168
Oldroyd, James 130
Orfalea, Paul 118
Ou, Kevin 261
Pamperin, Tracy 221
Perillo, Donna 55
Port, Michael 58
Ramberg, Connie 99
Ramberg, Ken ix
Ramberg, Max 222
Randall, Tracy 106
Ray, Ramon 220
Richards, Lea 212
Ries, Eric 52
Rose, David S. 3
Roth, Carol 166
Rozelle, Arien 234
Saeed, Aysha 12
Savla, Dhenu 257

Schiff, Lewis 69

Schiller, Abbie 166

Schiller, Colin 140

Sellery, Bruce 90

Sethi, Paul 70

Shane, Deborah 229

Shapiro, Andrew 114

Shell, Jules 47

Sickles, Bob 134

Silverstein, Frank xii

Silverstein, Wendy 208

Sinek, Simon 21

Sittig-Rolf,
    Andrea 225

Sivers, Derek 105

Smith, Larry 87

Smith, Steven 33

Snyder, Danielle 106

Stamen Arrillaga,
    Justine 218

Strauss, Steve 143

Suster, Mark 4

Thompson, Leslie 28

Town, Phil 74

Trinder, Kenneth 98

Tsen, Ben 49

Turner Bitterman,
    Jennifer 202

Vecchione, Tom 112

Vindici, Valerio 16

Vogel, Neil 152

Wagner, Brent 246

Waksman,
    Karen 136

Wallach, Ari 225

Weeks, Rachel 61

Weinzweig, Ari 104

Weiss, David 25

Weiss, Matthew 58

Weltman,
    Barbara 93

Williams, Susan 61

Whalen, Ellie 94

Yair, Ashlie 149

Yecies, Laura 251

COMPANY INDEX

#SmallBizChat 220

1-800-Flowers 59

888-Red-Light 58

A.Y. Dzyne 149

AboutAirport-
   Parking.com 56

Advertising Red
   Books 70

Alltop.com 232

Amy's Kitchen 59

Ask the Business
   Lawyer 51

BackPocket COO 253

BarryMoltz 75

Behance Network 262

Berkus Press 45

Big Ideas for Small
   Business 93

Biz2Credit 239

Black Enterprise 70

BlitzMasters 225

*Book Yourself
   Solid* 58

Bosma Group 89

Bubbles Galore Car
   & Dog Wash 9

Butter Beans, Inc. 80

Bytecafe
   Consulting 157

CD Baby 105

Chaiken Clothing 108

Charmed Life
   Products 77

CitiStorage 154

Clairemont Commu-
   nications 88

Clearbrook Farms 138

ClearRock
   Capital 181

Clif Bar &
   Company 27

CNET 251

Comfort restau-
   rant 13

Concrete Products
   Cooperative 242

Cooking.com 101

Credit Consulting
   Services 97

Customer
   Perspectives 54

DANNIJO 106

Day of Games,
   The 246

DeborahShane
   ToolBox.com 229

DODOcase 205

DoSomething.org 224

Duke Marketing 206

Duke University 128

Empower Consulting
   Group 191

Enchantment 232

*Entrepreneur
   Equation, The* 166

*Entrepreneur
   magazine* 216

EOS Surfaces 98

ExpertConsensus
   125

Fab.com 6

Fancy Food
   Show 138

Fav's Treatery 123

FeelingAnxious
   PR 234

FinancialWoman 82

First Round Capital 5

Form Pilates 212

Foundation
   Rwanda 47

Friendex 50

Galpin Motors 126

Gensler 112

Gilt Groupe 99

Good Solutions
Group 200

GoodSearch ix

Gotham Software 140

Government-
Auctions 35

GreenOrder 114

GrowBiz Media 145

GRP Partners 4

Guerin Glass
Architects 76

Gyrobike 204

Hair Rules 119

Harris Interactive 37

Harvard Business
School 63

Heather Lopez
Enterprises 192

Highly Relevant 250

Hipiti 85

Hit Your Stride 230

Home Depot,
The 135

HubSpot 2

Huffington Post 199

Hummingbird
Group 222

Hyde 129

Hypno Happy 174

Ideal Cost 182

IFX Forum, Inc. 39

Imperial Billiards 16

Influence At
Work 203

Influence: The
Psychology of
Persuasion 160

Internet Week 152

Ivy Cohen Corporate
Communica-
tions 30

JobTrak 99

Kaufman, Kaufman
& Miller 162

KEEN 114

Kepler's Books 13

KEV!NOU // PHO-
TOGRAPHY 261

Kikucall 34

Kinko's 118

Knobbe, Martens,
Olson & Bear 25

LaBonne's
Markets 54

Ladies Who
Launch 172

Lake 5 Media 165

Lead from Within 98

Lean Startup, The 52

Long Beach
Hydrobikes 175

Lumenere 261

Make Mine a Million
$ Business 253

Making Ideas
Happen 262

Marks Group,
The 244

Mary Kay 128

Mavens &
Moguls 158

Miss Jenny's
Pickles 150

Moman Sales 157

Monitor Group,
The 122

Moolala 90

Moss & Boris 92

Mother Company,
The 166

National Cooperative
Business Associa-
tion (NCBA) 242

New York Angels 3

New York Enterprise
Report 124

Obsidian Launch 153

Om Aroma 213

Organizing from the
Inside Out 264

Pacific Advancement
Partners 164

Paperlinks 178

Parties That Cook 82

Party Goddess!,
The 187

Payback Time 74

Peak Design 84

Pig of the Month
BBQ 212

Pilates on Fifth 159

plura Financial
Solutions 86

Predictable
Success 186

Premier Sports &
Entertainment 216

Product for Profit 136

Promoting Group *121*

PublicStuff *5*

Pumpkin Plan, The 153

Pure Energy Partners *238*

Purpl Media *175*

Raise The Bar *233*

Rich, Intelisano & Katz *79*

S3 Agency *71*

Samuel Adams *69*

Savor the Success women's network *213*

School House *61*

Scorpio Ventures *214*

Seventh Capital *15*

Shark Tank 17

Sickles Market *134*

Simple Sugars *77*

SkinnyScoop *168*

SKK Graduate School of Business *130*

Small Business Advocate, The 62

Small Business Bible, The 143

Smallbiztechnology.com *220*

Smalltownmarketing.com *210*

SmartyPants *168*

SMITH Magazine *87*

Solas Fashion *196*

Spectrum Management Group *28*

Sprayology *94*

Start with Why 21

Stash Tea *33*

Steven Smith Teamaker *33*

Strategic Law Partners *31*

Strategy and Tactics of Pricing, The 132

Succeedasyourownboss.com *220*

SugarSync *251*

Summit Service & Associates *171*

Summit Telecom *239*

SurveyMonkey *176*

SwagatUSA *257*

Sweet Lily *55*

Synthesis Corp. *225*

Tax Solutions *123*

Tazo Tea *33*

TEAK Fellowship *218*

Thanexus, Inc. *243*

TOMS *81*

Tough Mudder *46*

Transition Consulting Group *255*

TZG Partners *xi*

uc, THE SOURCE *228*

Uptown Soap Co. *26*

Urban Muse, The *221*

Webby Awards *152*

Weiss & Associates *58*

Wharton School *183*

What to Ask the Person in the Mirror 67

Woopaah *172*

Worry Proof MD *254*

Woven *180*

WS&A Communications *208*

Yale University *128*

Young Entrepreneur Council *236*

"Your Granny Geek" *25*

Zingerman's Delicatessen *103*

Zipcar *66*

**BUSINESS
PLUS**

Recognized as one of the world's most prestigious business imprints, Business Plus specializes in publishing books that are on the cutting edge. Like you, to be successful we always strive to be ahead of the curve.

Business Plus titles encompass a wide range of books and interests—including important business management works, state-of-the-art personal financial advice, noteworthy narrative accounts, the latest in sales and marketing advice, individualized career guidance, and autobiographies of the key business leaders of our time.

Our philosophy is that business is truly global in every way, and that today's business reader is looking for books that are both entertaining and educational. To find out more about what we're publishing, please check out the Business Plus blog at:

www.bizplusbooks.com